SO-DUV-686

CONCILIUM

Religion in the Eighties

CONCILIUM

Editorial Directors

Guiseppe Alberigo	Bologna	Italy
Gregory Baum	Toronto	Canada
Leonardo Boff	Petrópolis	Brazil
Antoine van den Boogaard	Nijmegen	The Netherlands
Paul Brand	Ankeveen	The Netherlands
Marie-Dominique Chenu O.P.	Paris	France
John Coleman	California	U.S.A.
Mary Collins O.S.B.	Washington	U.S.A.
Yves Congar O.P.	Paris	France
Mariasusai Dhavamony S.J.	Rome	Italy
Christian Duquoc O.P.	Lyon	France
Virgil Elizondo	San Antonio, Texas	U.S.A.
Casiano Floristán	Madrid	Spain
Claude Geffré O.P.	Paris	France
Norbert Greinacher	Tübingen	West Germany
Gustavo Gutiérrez	Lima	Peru
Peter Huizing S.J.	Nijmegen	The Netherlands
Bas van Iersel S.M.M.	Nijmegen	The Netherlands
Jean-Pierre Jossua O.P.	Paris	France
Hans Küng	Tübingen	West Germany
Nicholas Lash	Cambridge	Great Britain
René Laurentin	Paris	France
Johannes-Baptist Metz	Münster	West Germany
Dietmar Mieth	Düdingen	Switzerland
Jürgen Moltmann	Tübingen	West Germany
Roland Murphy O.Carm.	Durham, N.C.	U.S.A.
Jacques Pohier O.P.	Paris	France
David Power O.M.I.	Washington, D.C.	U.S.A.
Karl Rahner S.J.	Munich	West Germany
Luigi Sartori	Padua	Italy
Edward Schillebeeckx O.P.	Nijmegen	The Netherlands
Elisabeth Schüssler Fiorenza	Hyattsville, Md.	U.S.A.
David Tracy	Chicago	U.S.A.
Knut Walf	Nijmegen	The Netherlands
Anton Weiler	Nijmegen	The Netherlands
John Zizioulas	Glasgow	Great Britain

Lay Specialist Advisers

José Luis Aranguren	Madrid/Santa Barbara, Ca.	Spain/U.S.A.
Luciano Caglioti	Rome	Italy
August Wilhelm von Eiff	Bonn	West Germany
Paulo Freire	Geneva	Switzerland
Barbara Ward Jackson	London	Great Britain
Harald Weinrich	Munich	West Germany

Concilium 142 (2/1981): Liturgy

THE TIMES
OF
CELEBRATION

Edited by
David Power

English Language Editor
Marcus Lefébure

T. & T. CLARK LTD.
Edinburgh

THE SEABURY PRESS
New York

ARCHBISHOP ALEMANY LIBRARY
DOMINICAN COLLEGE
SAN RAFAEL, CALIFORNIA

230.2
T482

Copyright © 1981, by Stichting Concilium, T. & T. Clark Ltd. and The Seabury Press Inc. All rights reserved. Nothing contained in this publication shall be multiplied and/or made public by means of print, photographic print, microfilm, or in any other manner without the previous written consent of the Stichting Concilium, Nijmegen (Holland), T. & T. Clark Ltd., Edinburgh (Scotland) and The Seabury Press Inc., New York (U.S.A.).

February 1981
T. & T. Clark Ltd., 36 George Street, Edinburgh EH2 2LQ
ISBN: 0 567 30022 6

The Seabury Press, 815 Second Avenue, New York, N.Y. 10017
ISBN: 0 8164 2309 1

Library of Congress Catalog Card No.: 80 54384

Printed in Scotland by William Blackwood & Sons Ltd., Edinburgh

Concilium: Monthly except July and August.
Subscriptions 1981: All countries (except U.S.A. and Canada) £27·00 postage and handling included; U.S.A. and Canada $64.00 postage and handling included. (Second class postage licence 541-530 at New York, N.Y.) Subscription distribution in U.S. by Expediters of the Printed Word Ltd., 527 Madison Avenue, Suite 1217, New York, N.Y. 10022.

104211

CONTENTS

Editorial

WHEN THE title 'The Times of Celebration' was chosen for this issue of *Concilium*, it was not intended either philosophically or theologically, as if the issue promised a philosophy or a theology of time. The intention was more directly pastoral. The articles presented deal with times that people actually choose to celebrate, and not with some ideal pattern. The approach is both explanatory and critical.

The articles indicate four kinds of reason for which a particular season, day or hour is turned to celebration. One or other kind of reason may dominate, because of culture, faith or circumstance, but the four cannot in practice be totally separated from one another.

1. The habit of celebrating on a particular day may have no other root at a given time than a tradition or custom, rather blandly received by the living populace. The official teaching of the Church, or theology, may offer reasons for the tradition, but these are not necessarily perceived or received by those who follow the practice. Such seems to be the case, for example, with Sunday or Christmas for many Christians, both the pious and the not so pious. When this happens, the day or the season can be all too easily accommodated to the commercial or technical manipulation of time. Religious celebration then serves questionable social purposes.

2. In cultures where people live closely to nature, times for celebration have roots in cosmic, daily and seasonal, cycles. The symbolism of these cycles affects religious attitudes, and can continue to have a hold even in a technical age. The development of the Jewish and Christian calendars cannot be explained fully without reference to the seasons of the year. The rhythm of daily prayer follows the cycle of light and darkness. It is not the cosmic symbolism which determines the basic meaning of Jewish or Christian feast, but in practice one has to look into the meaning which it has for those who celebrate. Popular culture persistently gives rise to feasts at cosmic moments. The Church's calendar and daily prayer have accommodated this, even while teaching has insisted upon the central place of the non-cyclic Sunday or upon the commemorative character of the Pasch. In early centuries, there was a pastoral tactic of replacing pagan cyclic feasts with Christian commemorations, whether of Christ or of the martyrs and saints. The people often remained as much attached to the natural rites and symbols as they were to the Christian fact, and the two got interwoven. Even today, for example, it is interesting to note how important the rites of water and fire are on the feast of John the Baptist in some countries, and then to read the sermons of Saint Augustine for the feast, wherein he chastises the people for their pagan proclivities.

3. There is a further rooting of festive times in family occasions, often connected with the life passages of birth, adolescence, marriage and death. The practice of some of the sacraments has been largely attached to these, though of course the religious factor is only a part of a more extended celebration. Life passages apart, the reason why Christmas is the greatest popular feast in the Church's calendar seems to be that it is often celebrated by people as a family feast.

4. The reason for celebration which is specific to Judaism and Christianity is the event and its commemoration. The event of Christ's Pasch is at the heart of rites and prayers in Christian celebration. Other events, too, are marked in the calendar of feasts, both those pertinent to Christ's mystery and those which belong to the lives and deaths of the saints. Commemorating events is not without certain ambiguities. Questions can

be asked about the significance of some of the events whose commemoration has crept into the calendar over the centuries. The Church has instituted some feasts to commemorate victory in war. Other feasts have an appeal to the poor, since they commemorate some miracle or apparition which has significance for them. The intent is explicable as an effort to incorporate the Church's history into the history of the Christ event, but one has to ask whose history is thus being sanctified and what are the social implications of the celebration.

Indeed, when these four different kinds of reason for choosing times for celebration are noted, one has to pass on to a number of issues, which are in fact treated in one form or another in this issue of *Concilium*.

1. On a very practical level, one may ask what do people intend in fact to celebrate, since the Church's official position does not determine the answer to this question. In the articles here presented, Potel notes a frequent divergence between the ideas of the pastor and those of the people in celebrating the rites which mark life passages. Eicher indicates that the Sunday may in effect canonise a work ideal, quite opposed to the event which that day was instituted to proclaim. Aubry explains how we may read the language of the people themselves, as they express in their own rituals their sense of the place which they have in history and in society.

2. Consideration has to be given to the life-symbols, both cosmic and personal, that have been incorporated into Christian celebration, because of the times at which it takes place. This has practical implications for Easter and other feasts, since though they are celebrated on the same date in different parts of the world they are not everywhere celebrated in the same season. At a more theological level, the very important issue of the difference between cyclic time and historical time is raised. Both aspects are treated by Chupungco and touched upon by Talley and Dalmais, as well as by Duch and Aubry. The symbolism inherent in a daily rhythm of prayer is discussed by de Vogüé.

3. The necessity of rhythm to human nature and freedom in its use is another issue. De Vries indicates, for example, that whereas the Sabbath in Israel had been originally intended to celebrate freedom, under the priestly code it is used to ideological effect. Eicher makes us ask how tyrannical and ideological the observance of Sunday and the week-end have become in technological society, with the possible effect that the Christian assembly is not always in truth the keeping of the Day of the Lord. Treating of the rhythm of daily prayer in the monastic life, de Vogüé gives some general principles regarding both the limits and the usefulness of keeping time patterns of celebration.

4. The relation between the Church's universal calendar and particular calendars cannot be ignored. As Talley and Dalmais show, in the early origins of the now universal calendar some times or days were determined by local features and practices. The annual Pasch seems to be the only yearly feast of the Lord which is by definite intention attached to an actual date, however computed. Such a matter as the distinction between Christmas in the West and the Epiphany in the East is affected by local differences in the way of relating the Christian calendar to seasonal and non-Christian factors. In commemorating saintly persons or particular events, the place for particular calendars is obvious. Chupungco shows in his article that even when original and universal dates are retained, the symbolism which has cosmic roots cannot be the same for all climates. Keeping a universal calendar may in fact demand more divergence in the rites or prayers of a feast from one hemisphere to another.

5. The reductionism of Christian symbolism and celebration which occurs in the celebration of themes has to be faced and criticised. Present in the past in such feasts as Corpus Christi or the Sacred Heart, this tendency shows up nowadays in thematic celebrations of Peace, Justice, Communications, or in the ever-growing inclination of some groups to turn every occasion into a thematic display of words and ideas. This subject is discussed by Rennings, and it has much to do with the western tendency noted

by Duch to highlight logic and reason, in such a way that dogma and ethics become the major religious components.

6. How times of celebration and the forms in which a sense of time is expressed, relate to societal experience and reality is a major issue. In the gestures and modes of celebration, in the times at which they celebrate, in the events in which they rejoice, people express the way in which they feel they belong to society and to history. Eicher's discussion of the Sunday reflects on this. How did Sunday turn into a day of rest, when it was not that to begin with, but rather a weekday (in relation to Jewish and pagan time) and a workday on which Christians gathered to commemorate their liberation in the Lord? How do questions about celebrating the Sunday in industrial society, about its convenience or inconvenience, represent the sense that Christian communities have of time and of the dominant ethics of the society in which they live. The article written by Aubry may shock some readers on first reading, because of the facts which he narrates and the questions which he ponders. It is a very important contribution. The author points to the coexistence and even the conflict of different histories, of different senses of time, and to the fact that Church celebration can actually canonise domination, even while the poor retain their own ways of expressing their particular sense of history. In what he writes about recent occurrences in Nicaragua he raises the truly important question of how people with Christian faith, not in the past but in our own time, can live and celebrate political events within the horizons of history that are opened up in Christ.

In the lay-out of the issue, there are three articles which offer fundamental considerations on the choice of times for celebration. These are followed by six which deal with particular matters.

The article by Simon de Vries on time in the Bible can be taken as a point of reference for the whole issue, or as a kind of key to the reading of the other articles. The first few paragraphs of this article may seem rather technical, but they lead into very fundamental considerations. The author shows a variety of attitudes to time recorded in the Bible. These affect the choice of times for ritual, as well, they express the sense of history that people had. This explanation of the Bible helps towards an understanding of what happens in Christianity and sheds light on pastoral issues of the present day. Ideally, the Judeo-Christian perspective on time is that inspired by faith in the presence of the Lord in history, so that historical events become transparent to the Holy of that presence. Other human tendencies, however, are always at work in societies and communities, modifying the sense of history and showing up in the ways that choices are made regarding cult. Some questions seem to recur. Time has to be apportioned out so as to be used properly, but Christians are given the chance to live it as opportunity rather than as an entrapment. Ritual of its nature expresses reverence for the Holy, but this can degenerate all too easily into an inclination to turn God into a controllable presence. Taking history in earnest does not have to mean setting its limits in virtue of a transhistorical dualism, or reducing its outcome to one final, simple answer. History is to be celebrated in its openness to the special revelatory character of every day and of every event, and to the hope that God continues to work for us in Christ. Sacerdotal and non-sacerdotal tendencies in worship are inevitable, but freedom is retained when their fruitful tension is accepted.

In the second fundamental article, Thomas Talley traces the early history of the Church's calendar in such a way as to offer a Christian heortology, which points to the central significance of time in Christ. Lluís Duch then presents an anthropology of feast, showing how it expresses a sense of time. This allows the author to point to some of the contemporary problems of the manipulation of time. He contrasts a time sanctified by a religious attitude which is dominated by logic and productivity with a time which is lived in the memory of God.

x   EDITORIAL

In the first of the articles on particular questions, Anscar Chupungco discusses seasonal and cosmic symbolism in relation to the Christ event and to the choice of times for its celebration. I.-H. Dalmais then shows, in the light of history, and especially that of the eastern churches, how particular and universal calendars complement one another. Peter Eicher considers the place of Sunday in contemporary industrial society, and makes some suggestions which could give it a truly Christian significance for communities, which take social responsibility in earnest. André Aubry discusses the relation between social change and feast, as this pertains to the Third World and to the conflict in a sense of history which exists between the First and the Third World. Heinrich Rennings discusses the reduction of Christian celebration to an ideology through the domination of themes and the practical elimination of historical symbolism. Julien Potel writes about celebrating family events and about the Church's relation to these. Finally, Adalbert de Vogüé offers some considerations on the daily rhythm of prayer, as this is expressed in the monastic life, and in the contemporary renewal of the liturgy of the hours.

PART I

Fundamental Articles

Simon de Vries

Time in the Bible

IT IS NO longer necessary to ask whether the Bible has its own peculiar language of time. There are few informed scholars who would undertake to defend the misconstructions of Thorleif Boman, John Marsh and the Kittel Dictionary over against the penetrating criticisms of James Barr.[1] Sound linguistic methodology demolishes the notion that the Bible has its own sacred language. It is not biblical language, but the Bible's *use* of language, that is unique. Accordingly, it is not the biblical words for time, but the biblical understanding of what these words mean, i.e., the biblical perception of the factors that make time meaningful, that is distinctive.

There are, to be sure, specific vocabularies of time for both Hebrew (Old Testament) and the Greek (LXX, New Testament) Bibles. The leading words are:

'ēt: situation, time; *'attâ*: now
mô'ēd: appointed meeting, festival
yôm: day; pl. *yāmîm* = *'ēt*; *hayyôm*: today
rega': moment
qēṣ: end
'aḥªrît: future
qedem: past
'ôlām; *neṣaḥ* and *'ad*: remote or indefinite time

Χρόνος (*chronos*): time, duration
νῦν (*nun*): now
ἡμέρα (*hēmera*): day; σήμερον (*sēmeron*): today
καιρός (*kairos*): point of time, decisive moment, opportunity
αἰών (*aiōn*): age, indefinite time; αἰώνιος (*aiōnios*): eternal

The most important shift from Old Testament to New Testament usage, via the LXX, is to a quantitative connotation in the terms *chronos* and *aiōn*, essentially the contribution of apocalyptic ideology. LXX and New Testament *kairos* corresponds generally to the qualitative use of *yôm* in the Old Testament.

In the wide-ranging debate over the meaning of time and history for Christian theology, various polarities have been proposed, such as 'God's history' versus 'man's history', 'super-history' versus secular event, 'linear time' versus 'cyclical time'; but

3

none of these seems to be fully satisfactory. On the basis of the present writer's detailed examination of prominent terminology involving the Old Testament word *yôm*, 'day' in his book, *Yesterday, Today and Tomorrow, Time and History in the Old Testament* (Grand Rapids and London 1975), and in a number of related published articles, a more appropriate differentiation may be suggested. The only truly meaningful distinction that can be applied to the biblical data—one that is thoroughly scientific from the point of view of a comprehensive linguistic methodology—is that between what should be called a quantitative and a qualitative approach to the phenomenon of time. As we explain each of these, it will become apparent that it is the latter—the qualitative approach—that most centrally underlies biblical historiography, paraenesis, and eschatology, where the charismatic impulse comes to expression and where the central concern is with *Heilsgeschichte*, sacred history.

It is not implied that either of these approaches appears in isolation in any given genre of biblical literature. As a matter of fact, the two depend upon and complement each other. The question is, Which of the two predominates and is more central and decisive in those documents that provide the core of biblical tradition? Which of the two characterises most essentially God's action in human events and makes meaningful man's response in awareness of the transcendent imperative created by this action? The quantitative approach sees time as a succession of essentially commensurate entities—a given number of days or months or years. These temporal entities are susceptible to being spanned by the same measuring-staff, hence can be tabulated mathematically. This is time as a *quantum*, comparable to space (and, as Einstein showed, simply another dimension of it). The qualitative approach sees time as a succession of essentially unique, incommensurate experiences; for it, the day is an apprehensional unity, primitively conceived according to the event that gives it character.

One important thing to understand is that the word *yôm* has definite priority over other time-words such as *'ēt*, both lexicographically and literarily. That is, *yôm* is a pure time-word, even when used inexactly or metaphorically, whereas *'ēt* (usually translated 'time') refers first of all to a situation and only by extension to the specific time-element that may be part of a given situation. When we survey the combinations with *yôm*, we find very many of them within the historiographic and prophetic corpora but few of them in wisdom or apocalyptic. When we look for combinations with *'ēt*, on the other hand, we find fewer of them in the former and more of them in the latter. *Yôm* is sharp and specific, *'ēt* is generalising and vague; and the movement away from *yôm* to *'ēt* parallels the development within Hebraic literature away from historiography and prophecy onward towards wisdom and apocalyptic—two literary types that tend to generalise human experience and catalogue cosmic reality.

1. THE OBJECTIFICATION OF TIME

To understand our intended distinction, one need not depart from the etymology of the term 'qualitative' (Lat. *qualis*, 'of what sort') or from the etymology of 'quantitative' (Lat. *quantum*, 'how much'). When a unique or unparalleled event occurs, there is by definition nothing whatever to which it can be compared, hence the event in question becomes revelatory of 'the other'—even of 'the wholly other'—the Holy. But constantly the human mind strives to offset the dread of confronting something entirely unique by reducing it to categories of intellectual understanding, either by way of measurement or by way of comparison. Quantifying measurement enters into use as an abstractive process by which one 'time' is correlated with others purely on the basis of the passage of moving objects (the sun, moon, stars, timepieces, and the like) within a regular orbit or recurring routine. So also the qualifying approach that reduces temporal experience to analogies. Identifying a particular day for its special characteristics, the analytical mind makes intellectual and then linguistic comparisons with other days perceived to be somehow like it. Ultimately, all of life and history may be regularised and brought under control of man. The fact is that each unique historical experience, bordering on absoluteness and incontingency, nevertheless remains contingent and thus vulnerable to the levelling process involved in identification and categorisation. Separating and labelling reality is the essence of God's creative work as described in Genesis 1, but this represents equally as much the organising and controlling process that is followed by the human mind.

(a) Wisdom: analogical qualification

This is essentially what wisdom does. As may be seen in its various manifestations throughout the ancient Near East, as well as in the Old Testament, its constant aim is to manage reality by reducing its vast array of variegated phenomena to a complex set of rules. It remains instinctively optimistic that comprehensive understanding can lead to harmony and happiness. Searching for analogies amid distinctions, it strives to put all things into their proper framework and relate each item of experience to all other phenomena. Each human experience is viewed as exemplary in a positive or in a negative way, setting a standard for interpreting all applicable situations. Strikingly, the biblical wisdom texts seem to emphasise the distressing side of temporal experience. Borrowing from the language of historiography, to which the description of individual and collective disasters immediately belongs, wisdom sayings scattered through the Bible speak of a 'day of anger' (Job 20:28), a 'day of wrath' (Job 21:30; Prov. 11:4), a 'day of distress' (Job 21:30), a 'day of battle and warfare' (Job 38:23), and a 'day of slaughter' (Jer. 12:3). Especially common are combinations of yôm—especially in the plural—and 'ēt with the genitival qualifiers, rā'â, 'evil', and ṣārâ, 'distress'.

To Jesus ben Sira, the author of Ecclesiasticus, the Hebraic doctrine of creation came to mean that everything exists within a temporal pattern that is positively congenial to its salutory existence. Thus we read in 39:33-34 (see vv. 16-21):

The works of the Lord are all good,
    and he will supply every need in its hour (hōrā; Heb. 'ēt);
and no one can say, 'This is worse than that'
    for all things will prove good in their season (kairǭ; Heb. 'ēt).

Constantly, Sirach recommends such behaviour as is appropriate to the particular time, for it is the very essence of the wisdom impulse to correlate human actions with corresponding qualities of time. Yet, he warns that one should not become so totally absorbed in the prevailing conditions of a particular time as to forget that the situation may quickly change. As he says in Ecclus. 18:26, 'From morning to evening conditions change, and all things move swiftly before the Lord'. For Sirach, anxious to preserve divine sovereignty in human life, an awareness of change and temporality produces an attentive prudentialism in which, while God remains ever in charge of the course of human events, man feels himself obliged to respond appropriately, purposefully, and diligently, seeking an action that best suits the time.

For Qoheleth, the writer of Ecclesiastes, such an awareness only produces resignation. He acknowledges that there may indeed be a beneficent design in the way the creator has arranged his universe, assigning to each activity its proper time, but since man is unable to penetrate the curtain of divine inscrutability in order to trace the chain of cause and effect from beginning to end (Eccles. 3:11), man can secure no 'profit' for his toil and must content himself with such a modicum of happiness as God may allow him in the passing moment (Eccles. 3:9; and see 5:15, 17).

It is the notion that time is a trap (Eccles. 9:11-12), not an opportunity, that colours the interpretation of Qoheleth's catalogue in 3:1-8. One is interested to see that, although the Hebrew Bible employs a great variety of genitival qualifier with *yôm*, 'day',[2] Qoheleth avoids most of them. Individual days have now lost much of their significance, and Qoheleth is interested only in a pattern of opposing 'times' or situations. We observe two things in particular: (1) that comparative trivialities such as rending and sewing garments (perhaps also the enigmatic casting and gathering of stones)[3] are included among the more weighty matters, as though to encompass the totality of reality; also (2) that except at the end of v. 8 infinitival phrases (almost always with *le*) substitute for nouns in the construct chains that define the individual 'times'. This is striking, because elsewhere in the Hebrew Bible the infinitival construction with *le*, in reference to the word *'ēt*, expresses purpose—specifically, that of performing something not as yet occurring.[4] In other words Qoheleth is listing categories, not just of customary and habitual activities, but of teleologically directed actions—and by balancing the one against the other he seems deliberately to underscore a radical negation of purpose.

(b) Cultic language: cyclical quantification

So much for the qualifying objectivation of time in Israelite wisdom. The Israelite cultus was more interested in time as a quantum—the cyclical repetition of special days in a liturgical calendar. One example speaks for many: Leviticus 23 is priestly regulation for Israel's festivals, woven in a tight pattern of time-specifications, the concern of it all being to keep each element of ritual in correct sequence. What is to be done on each separate day is important, but still more vital is when what is done is done. It seems apparent that the priests were more prepared to think of time in quantitative than in qualitative terms. It is they who theologised about history as a chronological quantum, but most of their concerns were quite practical. They had to administer a calendar (to judge from Jubilees, I Enoch, Qumran, a subject of intense dispute within the priestly ranks) and regulate the cultic apparatus. It is they, therefore, who are found speaking of durations, of specific periods of time. When they define a particular day or time, it is with respect to its cultic character. Certainly the priests were very much aware of the distinctiveness of certain days, and especially of the great days of festival, for their greatest concern was to guard the sacred days, marking them off from all the other days on the calendar. But while they were ready to recognise—rather, eager to emphasise—the specialness of the holy days and seasons, they displayed little interest in unique historical event.

Within cultic religion an ideal, constantly recurring present may be seen as an abstraction from a mythical (or in Israel, quasi-mythical) prototype in the past. Numerous examples could be given, but none would be more impressive than the legislation for an historicised Passover-Mazzoth festival in Exod. 13:3-10. There Moses commands the people to remember *hayyôm hazzeh* ('this day' as nominal object) for its historical significance, but then immediately modifies this as a prohibition against the eating of leavened bread (v. 3). Next follows a prediction (with the participle and perfect-consecutives) of the historical 'going out' from Egypt and 'entering into' Canaan that are to take place on *this day* (vv. 4-5). This is followed in turn by a stipulation of the festival's seven-day duration (vv. 6-7) and by admonitions to teach and memorialise Yahweh's deed (vv. 8-9). The passage ends in a solemn command (v. 10) ensuring the observance of the festival in unvaried order (*lemô adah*, 'at its appointed time') and in perpetuity (*miyyamîm yamîmâ*, 'year after year').

(c) Apocalyptic: quantifying futurism with qualifying dualism

The common tendency to move from the unique to the universal, shared by cultic and by wisdom language, exemplifies an intellectual process of objectification showing significant similarities in both traditions, and if we carry our analysis a bit further we shall perceive an additional bond linking these two with apocalyptic. It may be said that, on the one hand, myth—perpetuated in ritual—and, on the other hand, wisdom, aim at reducing experiential reality to ultimate principles. Myth raises up prototypes within the primitive order of creation, while wisdom searches for a rational pattern within experienced reality. Israel was distinctive in its cultural environment in historicising its myth, but its ritual preserved the timelessness of myth. Israel was distinctive, too, in personalising the image of the creative principle standing behind experiential reality. But how does apocalyptic come in? We can surely perceive that under the impact of national disruption in its late history, Israel was led by its seers to transform what are essentially mythic images into the various patterns of apocalyptical dualism and futurism that come to greater and greater prominence in the post-exilic literature. It was thereby transporting the principle of ultimate meaning from a remote past or an idealised present to a future that interpenetrates the historical present, extending itself quantitatively beyond history as well.

Encompassing the entirety of the intellectual tradition, apocalyptic's ancestry included also the priesthood and the cult. Paul D. Hanson is mistaken, therefore, in his vigorous effort to prove that early apocalyptic was directed against the priestly establishment.[5] The influence of the 'Zadokite' priesthood is directly apparent in such emergent forms as Ezekiel's temple vision and the night-vision(s) of Zechariah, and it persists to a later period in the theology and protocol of Qumran. Objectification is manifest here as dualism, if not as futurism, though increasingly the two aspects appear together.

Like wisdom, apocalyptic ranges far and wide in search of an ultimate principle. Let us not be deceived by its seemingly encyclopaedic curiosity. It is not really interested in everything. It brings much in array that all may, if possible, be reduced to one final, simple answer. The ultimate failure of this effort is to be seen in the bitter despair of 4 Ezra. Qoheleth despairs because he gives up on history; the writer of 4 Ezra despairs because he continues, in spite of everything, to take history in earnest without knowing what to do with it.

Thus apocalyptic is not eschatological in the normative biblical conception. Applying an objectifying process of reduction to qualitative time, it produces a transhistorical dualism within the order of historical existence; applying a quantifying process of periodisation, it produces also a posthistorical futurism. Either way, it aims to identify ultimate meaning above or beyond history, freezing it into a state of absolute and final perfection.[6]

2. THE APPREHENSION OF QUALIFIEDLY UNIQUE TIME

(a) Historiography and prophetic eschatology

It was mainly the bearers of Israel's charismatic tradition—continuing from the time when the nation came into being, then passed on towards extinction, only to come to life

B

again as Yahweh's new creation—who recorded the significance of unique historical event. To them time is not a phenomenon that levels every human experience but something that lends it purpose and distinctiveness. Every day has its own special character. Every day is potentially revelatory. Every day presents a new choice, a new opportunity, a new responsibility. In each day man is at work, but God is at work too. This is the approach to time that in fact dominates the pages of the Old and New Testaments.

The essence of the qualitative, non-objectifying, apprehension of time is an awareness that God *has* done something 'from the beginning to the end'. One day is not simply related, numerically or categorically, to another day. Rather, each day is seen as transcendently significant in itself; i.e., each is seen as at least potentially revelatory of God's purpose. A day may be different from all other days, not only because it may be the occasion of a decisive event in the history of men and nations, but because it may be the opportunity for crucial confrontation between God and man.

The various days in the past when Yahweh has performed his judging and saving acts are memorialised in Israel's *heilsgeschichtliche* tradition. There was a day of Israel's election (Deut. 9:24; Ezek. 16:4f.), a day of plague on Egypt (Exod. 10:13), a day of crossing the sea (Exod. 12:17), a day (or days) of the giving of quails (Num. 11:32), a day for the dedication of the tabernacle (Num. 9:15), a day of the giving of the law (Deut. 4:10), a day of victory over the Amorites (Josh. 10:12). Many passages speak of Israel's greatest day, the day when Yahweh brought them out of Egypt (Judg. 19:30; 1 Sam. 8:8; 2 Sam. 7:6; Isa. 11:16; Jer. 7:22, 11:4, 7, 31:32, 34:13; Hos. 2:17; Ps. 78:42), while other passages mention days of Israel's past judgment (Num. 32:10; Isa. 31:15, 34:12; Hos. 10:14; Obad. 11, 14; Zech. 14:3; Ps. 78:9, 95:8, 137:7; Lam. 1:12, 2:1, 21f.; 1 Chron. 28:6), also days when Israel's neighbours received God's judgment (see 'the day Midian', Isa. 9:4). But there were new days of salvation for Israel (Hag. 2:15, 18f.; Zech. 4:10, 8:9), even as there are recurrent days of special relief for individual believers within Israel, celebrated in the psalms of declarative praise (Ps. 18:18, 20:2, 59:17, 77:3, 138:3, 140:8; Lam. 3:57). On this model, new, unique days of divine help and divine punishment can continually be expected. The greatest new day of divine judging and saving is the day of Christ's death and the day of Christ's resurrection (John 14:19-20).

It is important to understand that pre-apocalyptic prophetic eschatology is the situational counterpart of sacred historiography, projecting the future from the past, the unknown from the known. The Hebraic terminology of time reflects this correspondence; time for the Hebrews is more two- than three-dimensional. That is to say, to a greater degree than in western languages several identical words are used with reference to the future and the past: *'āz* and *bā'ēt hahî'* refer to unspecified time in the past or future; *bayyôm hahû'* refers to the time of a definite past or future event; *'ôlām* refers to remote time in the past or future. The past and the future are analogically related to each other, both being measurably distant from *'attâ*, 'now', *hayyôm*, 'today'—the present moment from which all human experience is viewed.

This enables us to see why prophecy cannot be divorced from historiography. Today's researchers know far better than previous generations of critics the extent of prophecy's indebtedness to the historical tradition. We now see that the prophets, specially admired by historicistic criticism for their irruptive novelty, stood very much in the midst of their people and the nation's situation, drawing from the past to elicit responsible behaviour in the present and in the immediate future. It is with this awareness that we must seek a solution to the Day of Yahweh problem and the entire question of eschatology. The transcendent surprise of Amos' speech about the 'Day of Yahweh' (5:18-20) lay not in the fact that there would be such a day or that Israel's god would come in judgment, but that his judgment would be a threat to Israel. Israel expected a decisive coming day because they remembered many decisive days in the past.

These considerations lead us now to make a confident surmise respecting the practical purpose of historiography on the one hand and prophetic eschatology on the other. Both have this identical pastoral concern: to awaken God's people in a present moment of crisis, calling them to repentance and decision—or, if the announcement be of God's saving purpose, to awaken them to trust and hope, the proper fruits of repentance. In other words, historiography and eschatology may be taken as forms of exhortation or paraenesis.

(b) Deuteronomic paraenesis

A third exemplar of the non-objectifying qualitative approach to time is the Deuteronomic paraenesis. It has become apparent to scholars using modern methodology that the long-fought-over book of Deuteronomy does not derive from the time of Moses but from a much later period. Following Albrecht Alt and Gerhard von Rad, we however join an emerging consensus in fixing its origin, not in Judah and in the reign of Josiah, as was held by Wellhausenian criticism, but in northern Israel shortly after the political collapse of Samaria. It is important to recognise a long and complex compositional process. Not only are there core materials—in particular, the lawbook—and late redactional elements, but one may discern distinct layers within the central paraenesis,[7] reflecting a situation of renewed confrontation between God and his people.

For Deuteronomy, each 'today' is crucial, though no 'today' is final. This is completely in accord with the time-concept of Israel's sacred historiography and explains also the meaning of prophetic eschatology. As God has had various decisive days in the past, he now renews the present day of decision. His action cannot be confined to one single time within history (a deistic, docetic notion) because every time may be his time of action. This is to say that every time is also man's moment of responsible choice since he stands constantly under the awareness that God will act savingly or judgingly according to his own—man's—response. This is history, God acting sovereignly in judgment and salvation; not in majestic aloneness but in intimate interaction with responsible man, each being bound to the other in mutual obligation.

Deuteronomy is thus a crystallisation of repeated paraenetical appeal, God's word ever renewed, continually calling man to choose life and blessing. The question that arises next is about its *Sitz im Leben*. In what formal setting and spiritual situation was the Deuteronomic paraenesis made? Artur Weiser, Gerhard von Rad, and others have speculated that Israel observed an annual covenant-renewal festival, but this has been questioned by those who have argued that no single biblical passage points unequivocally to it. Weak as the *argumentum e silentio* may be, it is nevertheless difficult to explain the Deuteronomic paraenesis on any other basis. It must be in some setting wherein the people presented themselves as morally responsible before God, and an authoritative spokesman ('Moses') presented God's demand and appeal, that it could have had any meaning. Whether or not its setting can be called liturgical may be decided, perhaps, through consideration of the very Deuteronomy-like appeal of Psalm 95. True, the covenant is not expressly mentioned here, but a covenant relationship and covenant obligation clearly are. This psalm is liturgy and a model for liturgy. In vv. 1-5 a priest/liturgist summons the worshipping congregation to praise Yahweh for his lordship over nature; then, in vv. 6-7a, renewing his summons, he shifts to a confession of the covenant bond. Suddenly, in vv. 7bff., the liturgist becomes a paraeneticist, plaintively appealing to the same worshipping, covenant-bound congregation to respond otherwise on the present day of decision than a previous generation had responded in another time and place: '*Hayyôm*—if you would obey his voice—do not harden your hearts as at Meribah, as on the day of testing in the desert!'

3. THE CELEBRATION OF REVELATORY EVENT IN BIBLICAL LITURGY

It is clear that paraenesis did have a place in Israel's formal liturgy, thus we cannot avoid inferring that liturgy was the proper setting for paraenesis whenever and wherever it occurred. This is true to some extent of prophetic preaching too. Though, without question, the prophets felt free to speak outside the shrine locale, we know that there were cult prophets and that every prophet had at least a theoretical right to speak in, to, or even against the shrines. This is to say that, while covenant paraenesis and oracular prophecy may at times have been forcibly excluded from liturgy—even from the cultic precincts—both had a normal, rightful role within it. How much of a role is hard to say. We may confidently suppose that sacrificial ritual continued to occupy the dominant place so long as the temple survived. But it was the recitation of sacred history, paraenesis, and oracular prophecy that preserved what was truly distinctive and constitutive in Israel's religion, namely, her awareness of Yahweh's past, present, and future action within her historical experience. Sacrificial ritual, based essentially upon a cyclical, quantitative control of time, celebrated that which is *timeless* in God. The *timely*, the unique, the historically revelatory were rehearsed in liturgical recitation or given current relevance in paraenesis and prophecy.

In which area, then, are we to place Israel's festival cult? First, let it be observed that strikingly little of the Old Testament's qualitative description of time turns out to belong to the ritual of the annual festivals. Second, let us ponder the fact that these festivals were calibrated to natural phenomena, namely, the cycles of the sun and moon and the agricultural seasons. They had indeed been raised up, to some extent, from pre-Yahwistic agricultural myth, and at least the Mazzoth/Passover feast had been historicised through an explicit association with the deliverance from Egypt. But even this festival represents a compromise as much as a triumph, exhibiting the tendency of cultic institutionalism to reduce the historically unique to something regularised and manageable. When the saving act of God comes to be memorialised in a sacramental ritual, it has subjected itself to a repetitive pattern that may lead, in the hands of small-minded defenders of the establishment, to mere repetition for its own sake. The divine may become confined within the apparatus of the sacramental cult, no longer challenging man to historical responsibleness before the sovereign demands of an omnipresent God, but soothing him with an assurance that God is somehow at his own disposal, elicitable through the correct cultic manipulation that is the secret of priests.

Some may wish to argue that biblical Israel never went so far as this. The claim is eminently debatable. Surely in primitive times numerous Israelites were, in fact, tempted by pagan worship, whose spiritual appeal has been carefully described in foregoing sentences. To what degree official Yahwism succumbed may only be inferred. Relevant texts are passages from the prophets in which the cult is denounced. Amos may have wanted to abolish it completely, though the majority of prophets attempted only to reform it. Was it because of its eclecticism that they thundered against it? A clue may be found in Jeremiah's famous temple sermon (chap. 7). Whereas the people thought that the temple and its ritual guaranteed Yahweh's favouring presence, Jeremiah knew that only their moral response to the covenant demand could guarantee Yahweh's favour, and thus preserve their temple. Prophecy understands all to well how the institutional cult may tend to stifle a personalistic religion. Convinced that Yahweh cannot be bound in ritual, that he can be obligated to no sacred place but works freely in every place and every time, prophecy calls the faithful to resist the temptation of resorting to 'rivers of oil' in the place of what is truly good, namely, 'Performing *mišpāt*, loving *hesed*, and living a reverential life before God' (Mic.6:6-8).

This, we affirm, was Israel's constitutive insight. Never completely lost, but ever preserved in the historiographic record and given new relevance within the charismatic tradition, it provided Israel with the one thing it needed to survive the loss of land, temple, and the entire political-cultic establishment. Once under Nebuchadrezzar, a second time under Titus, Israel had to fall back on the faith of the desert. With this, Judaism learned to survive the cruelties of history. Christianity, too, has often transcended deprivation of place, in spite of its susceptibility to rely upon the supports of cultic institutionalism.

The dilemma that unremittingly imperils the ongoing awareness of sacred history and the personalistic religion that goes with it is humankind's stake in politically and culturally stable systems. Unavoidably, some adjustment will have to be made if one is to live anywhere but in a formless waste. The practical problem, then, is how to keep a charismatic and morally responsive impulse alive while functioning within the structures of institutional society and institutional religion. Israel confronted this challenge first as it settled down into an agricultural society, surrounded by urban culture; its response was in the form of accommodation and assimilation, most of it helpful but some of it harmful.[8] The Canaanite shrines were taken over, with their sacrificial apparatus intact, along with their priesthood and some of their theology.[9] Thus Yahweh moved to the *Kulturland*. Israel came to confront a still more serious challenge when it abandoned the charismatic ideal of political leadership in favour of an institutional kingship and all that went with it. Now Yahweh was moved to Zion, where he remained installed until the ultimate tragedies of Israelite history jarred him loose. Yet the postexilic prophets were not able to abandon some form of the ancient ideal for restoring Yahweh to his resting place in Zion. The Ezekiel school had a new temple (chaps. 40ff.), accompanying the new heart (36:26). According to Malachi, Yahweh would come to remedy the scandal of desultory ritual within Jerusalem's restored cultus, not by destroying but by purifying it (3:1ff.).

We need to ask whether the Old Testament apprehension of sacred history finds a counterpart in the New Testament. Our observation is that the New Testament indeed stands essentially within the same qualitative, non-objectifying tradition. It is equally practical, situational, historically oriented, and morally concerned. Even as institutional-juridical, cultic, wisdom, and apocalyptic elements have developed as a subsidiary growth within the Old Testament canon, they can be shown to appear only on the fringes of New Testament development.

True, the New Testament is more eschatological than the Old Testament, but it has not, as a whole, fallen into the ahistorical orbit of apocalypticism, wisdom moralism, or cultic precisionism. It believes firmly that God has again acted in history, that he now involves his people and Church in a shared responsibility for history's outcome. The Church is given a charge to bring the gospel and win the world. Thus dominant literary elements within the New Testament are historiography (Gospels, Acts) and epistolography. It makes no essential difference whether the latter emphasises in any one place correct belief or moral behaviour (e.g., in Romans *versus* James) because both are directed towards the Church's present responsibility to respond to God's new saving act in Christ. Deuteronomy-like paraenesis is found in passages like 2 Cor. 6:1ff. and Hebrews 2.

Pondering the fact that the Old Testament genres bearing the *heilsgeschichtliche* tradition involve man in moral responsibility in the very act of recalling or predicting God's saving and judging work, it is difficult to believe that the New Testament appeal to trust in Christ may properly be construed in an antinomian way, as though the personal reception of the effects of God's work could ever have any consequence besides grateful and obedient moral living. If, indeed, New Testament sacred history is a genuine continuation of Old Testament sacred history, it must decisively affect the lives of those to whom the message of God's saving act is directed. Gospel historiography has a clear paraenetic purpose, motivating not only faith but the holy living that goes with it. When we read John 20:31, 'These are written that you may believe that Jesus is the Christ, the Son of God, and that believing you may have life in his name', can the life that results from faith mean anything different from the life that is promised in Deut. 30:15, a life that is joyfully fulfilled in the acceptance of covenant responsibility?

What has Christendom made of all this? To many adherents of the gospel, of whatever persuasion, Old Testament historiography has now (unfortunately) lost its authority because Israel's history is no longer received as relevant to the Church's history. It is the New Testament's sacred history, then, that moves the Church to pious thought and action, but in drastically different ways. The Christ event, however defined or restricted, means one thing to sacerdotal Christianity and quite another thing to non-sacerdotal Christianity. The difference has very much to do with time.

Very briefly we would describe the sacerdotal apprehension of the Christ event as rooted essentially in quantitative time. Sacerdotal ritual, participating in eternal life through sacramental manipulation and liturgical recitation, makes the sacred past present in a re-created Christ—a Christ made real not in hallowed memory but in metaphysical substance. Who can escape recognising here the same reduction of the timely to the timeless that we have identified in the cultic tradition of ancient Israel?[10] But all the difference in the world remains between a liturgical celebration that commemorates the past in order to motivate the faithful for responsible living in the present and future, and that which freezes both the past and the future into a timeless present without the urgent paraenetical appeal of the biblical exhortation.

The non-sacerdotal approach to the Christ event emphasises the uniquely qualitative element and preserves a strong sense of paraenetic urgency. It is, however, in grave danger of losing the transcendental reality of the sacred past through neglect of proper ritual. When the work of God in the past is allowed to recede to the level of pious recollection or sterile dogma, its power for motivating responsible action in the past and in the future is diminished.

If we read the Bible aright, we will learn to be responsive to God's work in time, both as a uniquely qualitative event and as a model for repetetive lifelong celebration. He who keeps these in dynamic tension will be successful in exemplifying the ideal of biblical religiosity.[11]

Notes

1. See particularly *The Semantics of Biblical Language* (Oxford 1961) and *Biblical Words for Time* (Naperville 1962).

2. See de Vries *Yesterday, Today and Tomorrow, Time and History in the Old Testament* (1975) pp. 42-50.

3. This reference is given a dubious sexual connotation in traditional Jewish interpretation; see R. Gordis *Koheleth—The Man and his World* (New York 1968). According to K. Galling, *HAT 18* (Tübingen 1940) p. 94, the reference is to 'dice', but this is far from certain.

4. Thus *'ēt lidrōš 'et-YHWH*, Hos. 10:12; *'ēt-bēt YHWH lĕhibbānôt*, Hag. 1:2; *'et . . . lāšebet bĕbāttèkem*, Hag. 1:4; *'ēt la'ăśôt la YEWH*, Ps. 119:126.

5. *The Dawn of Apocalyptic* (Philadelphia 1975). Hanson relies heavily on sociological principles in dividing between the 'Zadokite' priests as the 'haves' and the apocalypticists as the 'have nots', denying that Ezekiel and the night-vision(s) are in fact apocalyptic. Hanson barely mentions Ezekiel 38-39 and does less than justice to the important analysis of O. Plöger *Theokratie und Eschatologie* (WMANT 2; Neukirchen-Vluyn 1959), which identifies prominent elements of

dynamic tension within the heterogeneous movement associated with the priestly programme of the restoration period. The appeal of Hanson's argument lies in the unquestionable fact that the estranged and the desperate instinctively do turn to apocalyptic as a vehicle for expressing their aspirations. Its weakness lies in the failure to recognise that priests could be disillusioned too. One must allow for a disparity between priestly ideology, which may include eschatological elements (see P), and reductionistic tendencies within all institutions, including the cult.

6. This is especially apparent in Zechariah 14, where 'the last great Day of Yahweh has been crammed with everybody's dream and stretched into an era of endless bliss' de Vries, p. 308; see 325, 329 on use of the very *HYH*, 'to be' with *bayyôm hahû*.

7. See N. Lohfink SJ *Das Hauptgebot: Eine Untersuchung literarischer Einleitungsfragen zu Dtn 5-11* (Rome 1963).

8. Cf. G. von Rad *Old Testament Theology* (New York 1962) I pp. 15ff.

9. Cf. H.-J. Kraus *Gottesdienst in Israel*[2] (Munich 1962) pp. 160ff.

10. We discern in current debate concerning Christ's presence in the Eucharist that much Roman Catholic theology wants to find an orientation closer to the Protestant than the Eastern Orthodox conception. In this, Rome is the true mother of its daughter. The Reformation could never have come from Orthodoxy; it had to come from Catholicism.

11. The preceding article is an adaptation from S. J. de Vries, 'Deuteronomy, Exemplar of a Non-Sacerdotal Appropriation of Sacred History' in *Grace Upon Grace, Essays in Honor of Lester J. Kuper* ed. J. I. Cook (Grand Rapids 1975) pp. 95-105 (originally developed as a Colloquium paper at the Ecumenical Institute for Advanced Theological Studies, Jerusalem, April 1973), and from S. J. de Vries, 'Observations on Quantitative and Qualitative Time in Wisdom and Apocalyptic' in *Israelite Wisdom, Theological and Literary Essays in Honor of Samuel Terrien* ed. J. G. Gammie (New York-Missoula 1978) pp. 263-276.

Thomas Talley

A Christian Heortology

THE CELEBRATION of an annual cycle of festivals is a religious characteristic shared by Christians with most of mankind. As with most matters liturgical, it is the result not of an ecclesiastical constitution but of an evolution whose roots are often beyond the reach of the historian. The data, when they become visible, are rich to the point of confusion, and there is little concerning the liturgical shaping of times which is not open to scholarly dispute. Since the scope of this present essay will not admit of a responsible review of that evidence and its interpretations, a glimpse towards those roots demands a selectivity and a disciplined imagination which, defensible or not, must be acknowledged.

1. NEW TESTAMENT ARTICULATION

A Christian theology of festival must be prepared to encounter at the outset a certain ambivalence towards the cultic articulation of time in the New Testament and particularly in St Paul. Although the context in which he writes does not yet suggest a Christian adaptation of the Jewish Passover, he feels no diffidence in saying, 'Christ, our paschal lamb, has been sacrificed. Let us, therefore, celebrate the festival . . .' (I Cor. 5:7-8). While this may reflect his own continuing observance of Passover, he is careful to assure the Colossians that they are free from judgment by others in such matters as 'a festival or a new moon or a sabbath' (Col. 2:16). More negative is his disappointment at the continuing significance of ritual times for the Galatians whose observance of days and months and seasons he seems to regard as a return to paganism (Gal. 4:10). While this chiding may seem more harsh than his words to the Colossians, the point is the same: the present reality of Christ consigns all such observances to the realm of shadows, whether types that are fulfilled in Christ or the deeper shadows of those that are not gods.

Still, there is a frequently noted difference between the time sense which lay behind the cult of the gods and that which informed Jewish liturgy. The myths which presented the contents of pagan festivals did not refer to events within history but were rather situated at the time of the beginnings of all things, *en arche*. The cosmogonic ritual, as analysed by phenomenologists of religion, seeks to escape the mounting influence of the past—what Mircea Eliade calls, 'the terror of history'—by the ritual expulsion of malign influences (sin, disease, etc.) and the regeneration of time through the repetition of the cosmogony. The regular return of such festivals marks a 'death' and 'rebirth' of time itself, and thus points to such a cyclical view of time as was characteristic of Greek thought and which Eliade has described as, 'a refusal of history'.[1]

For biblical tradition, on the other hand, history itself is the locus of God's action. Time, in the biblical view, is defined by its beginning (creation) and its end (the *parousia*), between which stretches the line that is the locus of God's redemptive activity. This is true for both the Old Testament and the New, but with the radical difference that for the New Testament the central focus of history is no longer the *parousia* at its term, but the life and work of Jesus Christ, a shift of the centre of history which gives Christianity its familiar tension between the victory which already is and that which is to come. While the historical uniqueness of Christ's redemptive activity at that centre is fundamental, for early tradition that is not to be viewed only as an incursion *ab extra*, but as the climax of the historical process. Dietrich Ritschl has pointed out how the gnostic circular journey of the Logos, from the highest God down to the human realm and thence back to God, was 'opened' by Theophilus of Antioch to the curve which runs from creation to the eschaton, all the path of the journey of the Redeemer who is revealed by the resurrection at the centre to be the Lord of history, encompassing it and present to every moment of it.[2]

However strong such a linear understanding of time might be, it can be experienced only in cycles. Judaism makes the weekly cycle central to the covenant and the Genesis cosmogony roots the Sabbath in the very origin of the world, a weekly rest which replicates the completion of creation in the beginning. Neither this nor the observance of daily, monthly or annual cycles obviates the Jewish sense of the movement of history from creation to *parousia*. Rather, such cycles serve to articulate that history and to provide the framework for the people's memory and hope. Mere duration cannot be experienced as history. What is characteristic of the biblical sense of linear time is not a refusal of periodic festivals, but its assimilation of them to the history of Israel, filling them with the memory of God's redemptive activity and hope for the final victory.

That sense of history and eschatology was not nullified by the radical impact of the resurrection for Christ is the beginning and the end. However powerful the concern of the primitive Church with the presence of the risen Lord, a presence realised especially in the liturgical assembly, still St Paul's account of the Eucharist in I Cor. 11 reflects a sense of both past (*anamnesis*) and future ('until he comes') as realised in the Eucharistic proclamation. The presence of the Lord does not stand over against but rather includes both memory of the *ephapax* (one-for-all) redemptive act and hope for the fulfilment of history in the *parousia*. The Eucharist itself, whenever it is celebrated, is an actualisation of the Christian understanding of time. It is in this context that Cyrille Vogel observed that it is less surprising that the Christian Year developed so late than that it developed at all.[3] As it did develop, this original time sense in the Eucharist was at the heart of it, and, whatever else is to be said, Christian festival is an occasion of Eucharist.

It seems clear that the Eucharistic assembly of the Church was situated on the first day of the week well before the end of the first century, and many writers see that custom already in such texts as Acts 20:7-12 and I Cor. 16:2. The reference to 'the Lord's day' in Rev. 1:10 may represent an assimilation of the Christian eschatological expectation to the Old Testament 'Day of Yahweh', but that should not be opposed to the usual understanding of it as reference to the first day of the week, consistently known as 'the Lord's Day' from that point forward. Such eschatological reference did contribute to the designation of Sunday as the Eighth Day from the first half of the second century, although that points as well to the resurrection day as the first day of a new creation. That day, memorial of the beginning when the divine *Fiat lux* inaugurated creation and history, became in early Christian tradition both celebration of the first day of the new age inaugurated by the resurrection and prolepsis of its fulfilment in the final *parousia*.

While the exclusion of Christians from the synagogue and liturgical development in the Eucharist would lead eventually to a polemic which opposes Sunday to the Sabbath, it should be observed that it is the week determined by the Sabbath which is the fundamental framework of the Christian articulation of time, and the earliest observance of Sunday is not opposed to the observance of the Sabbath rest. While the Sabbath was an important occasion for the daily synagogue liturgy, it was not that which constituted the peculiarity of that day, but rather the commandment of rest which did not attach to the observance of Sunday by Christians. Even after the exclusion from the synagogue, the Sabbath continued to be a day on which fasting was not allowed, although Rome's deviation from that rule was a source of conflict already in the time of Tertullian. What constituted the singularity of Sunday in Christian observance was the Eucharistic assembly, known as 'the Lord's Supper' already in I Cor. 11:12, a phrase in which many see the reason for the designation of the day as 'the Lord's Day'. This celebration of the morrow of the Sabbath represents not a rejection of the covenant cycle, but a renewal of it in light of the resurrection. Confident that they gathered in the presence of the risen Lord and watching expectantly towards his imminent *parousia*, the earliest community found the week a sufficient frame for the ordering of its prayer and fasting.

2. PASCH

From this, however, one should not conclude that early Christians became instantly oblivious to the annual observances which surrounded them, however the resurrection faith may have mitigated the importance attached to such festivals. While, as suggested earlier, it seems unlikely that St Paul's reference to 'Christ, our paschal lamb' is itself an allusion to a Christian adaptation of that festival, it may well have been written in the context of the Jewish observance, and his further statement that he intends to remain in Ephesus until Pentecost (I Cor. 16:8) makes it clear that he was far from insensitive to the great feasts of the Jewish year. His allusion to Passover, in particular, establishes his familiarity with the tradition that it was at Passover that Christ was crucified. Indeed, if his words are given their full value, he is aware of that tradition which lies behind the passion chronology of the Fourth Gospel. Whatever position one might take on the relative historical merits of the conflicting chronologies of John and the synoptics at that point, it seems clear that it was the synoptic tradition which exerted the deeper influence on the development of the Eucharistic prayer. On the other hand, it seems to have been the chronology of John, situating the crucifixion on the *paraskeve* of Passover at the time of the slaying of the lambs for the feast, which was to exercise determinative influence on liturgical time through the emergence of a distinctively Christian celebration of Pasch as the first and still pivotal observance of a Christian year as distinct from the earlier Christian week.

While the discussion of the origins of the Christian Pasch seems sure to continue, the clear tendency of the recent literature is to recognise the Quartodeciman Pasch as the original form of the observance, rather, than as only a local variant of an annual festival kept elsewhere on Sunday from the same period.[4] It is easy to understand the transition from the observance of the Passover of the Law by Christians to the Quartodeciman Pasch. That would involve no more than lengthening the fast on the anniversay of Jesus' passion to extend through the hours of the Jews' rejoicing and replacing that festive dinner with the more solemnly joyous Eucharist. On the other hand, it is difficult to understand what it would mean to raise one Sunday to the status of an annual festival whose content so nearly corresponds to that of every Sunday. Therefore, the most satisfying solution to the problem of the early Pasch is that it took its beginning from a deepening sense of the inappropriateness of such festivity as the Passover entailed in the face of the memory of the passion, so that that day was spent in fasting resolved in the Eucharist in the end of the night. From the end of the first century, probably, that fast distinguished 14 Nisan from all other days of the year, so focused upon commemoration of Christ's passion as to suggest to writers of the second century that the name of the observance, Pasch (actually derived from the Hebrew *pesach*), came from the Greek verb meaning 'to suffer' (*paschein*). In spite of that, Pasch was nonetheless a unitive celebration of Christ's *ephapax* redemptive work, and the fast was ended in celebration of his exaltation. In areas where the Church was not confronted so directly with the Jewish celebration of Passover, the force of the original hebdomadal pattern made this concluding Eucharist seem better situated on Sunday, already the weekly occasion for the celebration of the resurrection. The one-day fast became an exception to the normal resistance to Sabbath fasting and often appeared as the second day of a two-day fast through is juxtaposition to the regular Friday station. That fast, now concluded towards cockcrow on Sunday morning, still characterised the total observance, and Origen (*Hom. on Isa.* 5.2) can speak of this Sunday as that which commemorates Christ's passion, by contrast to the celebration of the resurrection every Eighth Day.

This adjustment of the paschal observance to the structure of the week, compounded by the Christian replacement of the fundamentally lunar calendar of normative Judaism with the solar calendar of Egypt and the Roman Empire, gave the Pasch a movable character which would receive further precision at the Council of Nicea. This movability, however, should not be allowed to obscure the nature of the original observance. It was the anniversary commemoration of an event (the crucifixion) on the *known date* (according to the lunar calendar) of its original occurrence. Whatever the complexities attending later computation of the date of Easter, that seminal annual observance was first rooted in the Church's historical memory of the *ephapax* work of Christ, a memory drawn into annual observance by the lengthening of the Church's past.

It is that same reference of Pasch to the passion of Christ which moved Tertullian to assert that, while any time is appropriate for baptism, the most solemn time is the Pasch and the following pentecost. This earliest clear reference to paschal baptism almost surely has Romans 6 in view, and that theology of baptism as participation in Christ's burial and resurrection led to almost universal celebration of baptism at Easter by the fourth century. At Rome, especially, the rites of initiation were bound to the paschal observance (with Pentecost as an option for those prevented at Easter), and any other time for solemn baptism was strongly resisted right into the high middle ages. While in other churches other festivals would become occasions for solemn baptism, it is not clear that these were preceded by the same process of final formation as Lent provided for Easter baptisms and the appearance of such baptismal festivals seems to parallel the increase in baptism of young children. Nonetheless, while Alexandria seems to have been slower in coming to it than other churches, Easter was the baptismal festival *par excellence*, and from the third century that baptismal function played a major role in shaping the paschal feast and preparation for it. Through baptism the Pasch became more than memorial of Christ's death and resurrection, for that *ephapax* redemption was sacramentally accomplished *ephapax* in those who by baptism passed into new life.

For the very early Church, however, participation in Christ's passion was not limited to that sacramental experience. Tertullian (*De bapt.* 16) was but one of many who linked baptism to the passion of the martyrs, their suffering being such a participation in that of the Lord that their death could only be spoken of as their triumph. Martyrdom and the whole engagement of Christianity with the powers of this world which occasioned it were seen as testimony to Christ's lordship over history. From as early as the martyrdom of Polycarp in the middle of the second century, the funeral practice of the ancient world with its tradition of periodic visits to the tombs of the departed would present to the Church commemorative feasts which celebrated this or that disciple in whose life and death the triumph and abiding presence of Christ in history was manifest. In many instances, growing density in the calendar would lead to the transfer of some saints to other days, but even then it is clear that the veneration of the martyrs was rooted in the celebration of datable events on the anniversaries of their occurrence, as was the Pasch in its origins.

3. BEGINNING OF THE LITURGICAL YEAR

That original annual observance established the year as a liturgically sensitive cycle for Christianity, but it did not immediately furnish the year with an integrated cycle of festivals of Christ. Even the fifty days of paschal rejoicing resisted conformation to the Lukan chronology of the ascension of Christ and the descent of the Spirit until late in the fourth century. Pasch is the centre of the year as Christ is the centre of history, but the establishment of that centre did not define a distinctively Christian beginning of the year. Two documents of the fourth century indicate two solutions to that need. The Chronograph of 354 at Rome begins its calendar of martyrs' commemorations with the notice of Christ's birth at Bethlehem against the date of 25 December, thus indicating that date as the head of the year. Additions to the parallel list of bishops' commemorations put the compilation of the original list no later than 336. 25 December, taken as standard for the winter solstice in the Julian reform of the Roman calendar by the Egyptian astronomer, Sosigenes, became the *natalis solis invicti* established by Aurelian's dedication of a temple to the sun in the Campus Martius in A.D. 274. As the Christian *natalis solis iustitiae* from at least 336, it was the celebration of the nativity, the *adventus* of Christ, which Leo in the fifth century would refer to as *sacramentum incarnationis*, although (to his considerable consternation) popular custom still revered it as the birthday of the sun, the day on which the shortening of the hours of daylight was reversed and the sun again began its ascendency over darkness. Indeed, the gospel of the Mass *in die,* the oldest of Rome's three Masses for the feast, not only proclaims, 'the Word was made flesh and dwelt among us', but also, 'the light shines in darkness and the darkness has not overcome it'.

Older than that Roman feast of the nativity is the Epiphany festival on 6 January which is indicated as the beginning of the year in the second document, the sixteenth of the *Canons of Athanasius,* an Egyptian compilation of the fourth century. There the Epiphany is recognised as one of three feasts of Christ in the year, along with Pasch and Pentecost. Of it the text says that it is the day on which the Lord was baptised by John, whence it is called the Feast of the Baptism, that Egyptians call it the feast of the beginning of the year, a new-year's day marking the ingathering of the harvest, and that in the same month (Tybi) the Saviour miraculously made water wine. About the same time, Egeria in Jerusalem writes of a seemingly well established feast (complete with octave) bearing the same name, Epiphany, and falling on the same date, 6 January. There, however, it is the feast of the nativity at Bethlehem, and there is no mention of any other theme. At about the beginning of the fifth century, Cassian will report that in Egypt both the nativity and the baptism are kept on the same day, and that may have been so in Athanasius' time, though it is most likely that the baptism was the original theme of the feast at Alexandria. Elsewhere in the later fourth century one or both of those themes will be found, and the miracle at Cana and even the transfiguration and the multiplication of loaves are encountered as themes of the feast, together with the adoration of the Magi either included with the nativity or distinct from it. Here, evidently, we are confronted with a feast celebrating not an event on the known date of its original occurrence, but rather the manifestation of Christ's divine power, the appearing of divine glory in history, as a concept exemplified in a plurality of events in the gospel. Indeed, in Gaul the feast will regularly celebrate the *tria miracula* of the adoration of the Magi, the baptism ánd the wedding at Cana. The concept of Epiphany itself is a rich one and Christine Mohrmann's classic study of it takes note of the close relationship between *epiphaneia* and *parousia* in such New Testament texts as 2 Thess. 2:8, a relation of the historical and eschatological appearances of Christ which continues in the Latin *adventus*.[5] It is a general characteristic of festivals of the beginning of the year that, as a threshold time, they suggest the end of time as well.

It has often been said that in the fourth century the early eschatological focus of liturgical time gave way to historical interest, but that becomes difficult to sustain when we compare the historical sensitivity of the primitive Pasch and memorials of the martyrs to the flowering of theological themes about these feasts of the turning of the year. Yet, Giles Quispel has warned against any such sharp disjunction between early and patristic thought on time,[6] and we must avoid any contrary disjunction that would suggest a radically new theological or even eschatological mentality in the fourth century. The development which proliferates about these feasts should be expected to be more continuous with the tradition and to be rooted in a more simple or even practical consideration. For such a plurality of themes, a plurality inviting further thematic elaboration, a simpler origin can be imagined, and may be worthy of consideration.

The Roman nativity feast on 25 December found wide acceptance in the East during the later fourth century, eventually finding a place in all calendars except the Armenian. Of those churches which did accept the new feast, however, Jerusalem and Alexandria resisted it longest.. At Jerusalem in the fifth century the nativity was still kept on 6 January, while at Alexandria in the same period the nativity had been joined to the original theme, the baptism, on this day which marked the beginning of the year. The reasons assigned to the choice of this date (6 January) are many and contradictory, but the most frequently cited in this century has probably been that of Eduard Norden who saw it as the date of the winter solstice at the time of the founding of the Middle Kingdom in Egypt.[7] While that explanation is not without difficulties in terms of Egyptian chronology, it does seem clear that that date was taken as a significant turning of the year, whatever the reason. As beginning of the year, it would be the beginning of a course reading of Scripture, including the course reading of a gospel. The beginning of the Gospel of Matthew is the nativity and the oldest Jerusalem lectionary not only shows Matthew to be the gospel read in Holy Week but betrays vestiges of a Matthean course reading in the Epiphany octave. The Gospel of Mark, on the other hand, begins with the baptism of Jesus and there are suggestions that that gospel was read in course at Alexandria. Studies by R.-G. Coquin,[8] based on medieval Syrian, Coptic and Alexandrian Melchite sources but supported by such earlier texts as the *Canons of Hippolytus* and (perhaps less securely) Origen's tenth *Homily on Leviticus*, argue that in ante-Nicene Alexandria the fast of forty days was begun on the day following the commemoration of Jesus' baptism on 6 January, thus following the chronology of the gospel. The richest, albeit the latest (fourteenth century), of Coquin's sources, *The Lamp of Darkness* by Abu 'l-Barakat, says that that feast was concluded with the Feast of Palms, celebration of the entry into Jerusalem (as in Mark 11), while the Pasch was observed 'at its own time in the month of Nisan'.[9] The final (sixth) week of that fast was the occasion for baptism, according to that and other sources, and a recently discovered document may afford confirmation to this very late description of very early Alexandrian usage. Purporting to be a letter of clement of Alexandria (a claim which many patristic scholars find supported by internal evidence), that document reports the use at Alexandria of a peculiar local version of the Gospel of Mark which contained a pericope not found in the canonical text but which was read, it says, 'to those being initiated into the great mysteries'.[10] That pericope followed Mark 10:34, therefore just prior to the account of the entry into Jerusalem which Abu 'l-Barakat put on the Sunday following the baptisms. After the account of that entry, the Gospel of Mark is virtually without chronological line until it takes up the passion narrative at chapter 14, as (on such an hypothesis) would have been the case with the liturgical year at Alexandria from the Feast of Palms on the seventh Sunday after Epiphany until the separately determined time of the paschal fast.

Allan McArthur has suggested that Epiphany originally united both the nativity and baptism in one festival through the influence of the reading of the beginning of the Fourth Gospel at Ephesus, and this would explain the prominence of the miracle at the Cana wedding feast.[11] In sum, such an explanation of the variety of early Epiphany themes by the differences between the gospels seems to me to be more satisfying than the supposition that themes were selected from this or that gospel because they reflected one or another aspect of the mythic content of a pagan festival on 6 January, especially in view of the sparsity of our evidence about any such festival. Some studies, the assessment of which would lie beyond the scope of this paper, have argued that the gospels themselves are meant to be lectionaries keyed to the readings in the synagogue. The most recent of these proposes the use of Matthew about a complete annual cycle, while Mark is taken to have contained lections only for the half year running from the beginning of the year (Tabernacles or Ingathering) to Passover.[12] The comparison of this hypothesis with the description of Epiphany as the feast of ingathering in the *Canons of Athanasius* would not bring forth the first suggestion of a connection between Epiphany and Tabernacles, but those suggestions have yielded no firm conclusions.

While, as suggested above, there is little indication that historical interest is new to the fourth century, there is a concern to give historical consistency to thematic pluralism and to extrapolate unknown dates from those that are established. Thus, the occurrence of the nativity and baptism on the same day is explained by reference to Luke 3:23, and from the nativity date on 25 December (once that was accepted) extrapolation from the winter solstice supplied themes to the other quarter-tense days: the conception of Jesus on 25 March, and the conception and birth of John the Baptist on 24 September and 24 June, the six-month displacement based on Luke 1:36. From the Lukan chronology would come also the celebration of the ascension on the fortieth day of paschaltide and the descent of the Spirit on the fiftieth. Unlike the annunciation and nativity whose true dates were unknown, these are based on the Pasch itself, and their slow establishment in the liturgical year suggests a measure of diffidence towards the Lukan chronology in the earlier tradition. Indeed, as Robert Cabié has shown, the ascension was first celebrated together with the descent of the Spirit as the seal of the paschal rejoicing.[13] This seems still to have been the case at Jerusalem in the penultimate decade of the fourth century.

CONCLUSION

In the Holy City the building of churches gave rise to still other feasts on the anniversaries of their dedications', and some of the more important of these achieved a place in the universal calendar. An important example was the dedication of Constantine's complex at Golgotha and the tomb of Christ, a location which seems about as precise as once was the date of the passion. That the date of the observance of that passion no longer pretends to calendrical accuracy is a function of the Church's original fidelity to the seven-day week as the liturgical cycle of the covenant in terms of which alone the day of resurrection, the new day of the new age, should be expressed. On that day the community gathered and gathers still in witness to and in communion with the risen Lord whose presence is focus of history remembered and the consummation for which we hope, both summoned in the Eucharistic presence. No 'terror of history' nor fear of an uncertain future finds place in that celebration week by week as the Church moves along the curve of history through the year which is history's type and ikon. Reflecting the journey of the Redeemer (which is as well that of his Church), the cycle of yearly festivals bears what memory has preserved towards the central Paschal Mystery, and from that, empowered by the Spirit, hope reaches out to the end. And in that end is our beginning.

Such, it seems to me, is the Christian understanding of time which shaped the gospels which shaped the liturgy. That this is not such a cyclical destruction and regeneration of time as the non-biblical religions know is due to the fixed point of our memory, the *ephapax* redemption accomplished on the Cross. It is that which destroyed 'the terror of history' and opens the future to hope, which made and makes martyrs' deaths to be triumph, and reveals the end of the world in the beginning of the gospel.

Notes

1. M. Eliade *The Myth of the Eternal Return* (Bollingen Series XLVI) (New York 1954) p. 117.

2. D. Ritschl *Memory and Hope: an Inquiry Concerning the Presence of Christ* (New York 1967) pp. 78-83.

3. C. Vogel *Introduction aux sources de l'histoire du culte chrétien au moyen âge* (Spoleto 1966) p. 264, n. 77.

4. M. Richard 'La Question pascale au IIe siècle' *L'Orient Syrien* 6 (1961) 179-212; W. Huber *Passa und Ostern* (Berlin 1969).

5. C. Mohrmann 'Epiphania' *Études sur le latin des chrétiens* I (Rome 1958) p. 252 ff.

6. G. Quispel 'Time and History in Patristic Christianity' *Man and Time: Papers from the Eranos Yearbooks* (Bollingen Series XXX) (New York 1957) pp. 85-107.

7. E. Norden *Die Geburt des Kindes: Geschichte einer religiösen Idee* (Leipzig 1924) p. 38.

8. R.-G. Coquin 'Les origines de l'Épiphanie en Égypte' *Noël, Epiphanie: retour du Christ* (Lex Orandi 40) (Paris 1967) pp. 139-170; 'Une réforme liturgique du concile de Nicée (325)? *Comptes rendu, Académie des inscriptions et belle-lettres* (Paris 1967) pp. 178-192.

9. Coquin does not refer to this passage. I take it from the French of L. Villecourt 'Les Observances liturgiques et la discipline du jeûne dans l'Église copte. IV: Jeûnes et Semaine-Sainte *Le Muséon* 38 (1925) 314.

10. M. Smith *Clement of Alexandria and a Secret Gospel of Mark* (Cambridge (Mass.) 1973) p. 446.

11. A. McArthur *The Evolution of the Christian Year* (London 1953) p. 69.

12. M. D. Goulder *Midrash and Lection in Matthew* (London 1974) pp. 171-201.

13. R. Cabié *La Pentecôte* (Paris 1965) pp. 117-178.

Lluís Duch

The Experience and Symbolism of Time

1. THE DESTRUCTIVE MARCH OF TIME

IN AN UNPUBLISHED work, issued by Henri Desroche in 1974, Roger Bastide stated: 'The possibility of Sunday does not exist for Prometheus'.[1] Sunday, the feast day in its broadest and most fruitful sense, seems to have no place in a modern age whose motto is 'Time is money'. This situation has a long pre-history, however, since it was the Greeks who gave the West its cultural hero in the shape of Prometheus, who forges civilisation not on the strength of a gift from the gods, as happens in Africa or Asia, but on the basis of the work of man's hands. So Roger Dadoun can write that 'western will finds its favoured expression in clockwork'.[2]

This attitude, we should remember, leads to the continual creation in western history of 'others', those against and from whom the correct, integrated behaviour proper to western man is defined. Heretics, witches, women, savages, homosexuals, drug addicts and so on have been the 'others' who, at any given moment in history, allowed the establishment of 'western reason' in a continuous process of unmasking.[3] The time of these 'others' was not *real time*, the time of doing, manipulating, 'working oneself out' as the subject of needs (Hegel). On the basis of the triumph of the time of the enterprise (*Gesellschaft*), and because of the impact of technical and economic language, the time of the community *(Gemeinde)* has been progressively reduced to more restrictive spheres. The churches have suffered the same fate, to the extent that, through incessant bureaucratisation in both doctrinal and moral spheres, they have generally forgotten their mission of anticipating the *space* and *time* of the *status patriae*. So the goal of history, the reconciliation of man with himself, with his fellows, with nature and with God, has ceased to operate within the framework of ecclesiastical institutions, with the result that other 'sociological settings'—which may be no less religious for being different—have frequently taken the place of the churches. Neither official religion nor science have kept their promises, since 'religion has lost its explosive elements and its illusions. Science, instead of freeing mankind from fear, has proved a powerful destructive force.'[4]

It is not only time that has suffered the impact of *homo faber*; space too has been equally subject to his progressive depredations, so that the machinations of all sorts practised on public space (cities, nature) can also be regarded as a *sui generis* creation of man's Promethean efforts. Space-time, which should be the ideal setting for *anticipation* of the desire for reconciliation of man with man, with nature and with God, has in fact become open ground for *experimentation*, leading sooner or later to the 'symbolic destructuring' of man (Willaime) and the 'inartistic behaviour' of the individual (Sennet). As Eugen Biser shows, 'dis-imagination' (*Entbildung*) has, from this standpoint, become the typical attitude of modern man.[5] This situation also has a fairly remote origin, when the West began to abandon the *image*, the symbol, as a genuine means of expressing religious experience and, almost exclusively, adopted the *concept* as the means of giving 'scientific' form to man's experience of space-time. Or, to put it slightly more gently: it was claimed that the 'logical word' could always replace the 'mythical word' in every way, thereby inexorably impoverishing the expressive capacity of the human being.[6]

2. TIME AND RELIGION

'Time suffers pangs of incarnation' (Octavio Paz)

Religion is a communicative activity within the bosom of the community. There is no need to wait for modern theories of communication to see religion as eminently a form of *communication*: it has always been this, because it has, for better or worse, always set up channels of communication among men. With which one has to point out that the communicative activity of religions has, in different spacio-temporal conjunctures, given rise either to the liberation of man, or to his enslavement and alienation.[7]

The communication established by religion forms part of a *process of transmission and re-creation* of what I have elsewhere called 'the origins and goals of the community'.[8] One has to bear in mind that the characteristics of a particular religious tradition cannot be reduced to mere repetition of the past, nor to the recreation, *ex nihilo*, of 'religious doctrine and behaviour'. The reduction of religion to its dogmatic and ethical components, which has been the dominant tendency in the last few centuries of Christianity, has fallen into one or other of the traps mentioned above: either ultra-conservatism or progressivism which denies its own religious tradition. Dogma and ethics reduce human expressive capacity to such an extent that, faced with the inevitable choice between *power* and *meaning* the first is inexorably chosen at the expense of the latter.[9] Religious communication, however, possesses another way, which I believe is the right one: transmission and re-creation of meaning through the multiple and often forgotten forms of human expressivity. Beyond its dogmatic and ethical dimensions, religion, in so far as it is *living religion* 'consecrates the moment' (Octavio Paz) in the form of genuine religious experience.

There is no doubt that 'present-day society throughout the world finds itself *increasingly subject to its own internal determinisms*'.[10] Cultural exchange takes place on a world-wide scale: the distinction between 'our own' and 'foreign', which formed the principal reference-point of pre-modern society, seems to dissipate with each passing day.[11] Many would claim that we are immersed in a world-wide culture which poses the same problems all over the world, problems requiring an identical response. Yet the 'right to be different' (Baladier, Sölle) is still something that must not be renounced either on an individual or a collective level, since loss of one's own tradition, actualised and re-created in the *here and now*, is the indispensable condition for achieving personal and collective identity.

As far as religion is concerned, this observation is of prime importance. *My* religious time cannot be reduced to an invariable, serial factor common to all mankind, one that can be lived and experienced in an identical manner in every part of the world. The same can be said for the time of *my* religious community. This, in effect, comes from a past, is living in a present, and is directed towards a future which all possess characteristics that

c

cannot be reduced to those of the 'times' of other religious communities. Dogma and ethics can—up to a point, at least—be common to all men and communities, particularly in an age of generalised communication such as ours, because thought and action can contain a certain similarity of tasks to be carried out. But, as I have already said, religion is not distinguished primarily by thought and action (though these are absolutely essential to it), but by an experiential way of living time, one which tends toward its abolition, when God may be 'all in all'. *Chronos* allows a wide base of supra-community and supra-personal encounter, but *kairos* demands a personal statement of the relationship between man and the foundation of his being. And, speaking 'religiously', one could say that encounter with one's fellows, taking on responsibility for them and the struggle for liberation that take place within the *chronos* of the world, are achieved to the extent that *homo religiosus* and religious communities fulfil the experiences of their own, identifying *kairoi*.

Faith is transmitted through a community language that operates on three levels: theological (conceptual), axiological (moral) and experiential (personal and identifying). It might be said that the expressivity of believers has been reduced almost completely to the two first levels. Ecclesiastical orthodoxies have struggled to bring their conceptualisations into line with 'the latest' scientific theories, whose patron saint, at least until the early part of the twentieth century, was *positivism*. This is the attempt to delineate what can be called human on the exclusive basis of verification as understood by nineteenth-century science. Apart from this, ecclesiastical systems made themselves increasingly technocratic and bureaucratic in order to achieve 'greater moral results' and 'more complete control' over believers. In this way, the experiential aspect of religion was relegated to a secondary place and very often subject to suspicion and condemnation. The preference theoretically shown to 'scientific discourse' and the requirements of absolutism attributed to 'practical Church affairs' have been powerful contributors to the dismantling of the symbolic so evident in the Christianity of our days. The transmission of faith in its theological (conceptual) aspect, carried out through 'manuals' in the seminaries and through 'catechisms' for the mass of the people, allowed for no re-creation either of a *community 'we'* or of *personal identity* in the members of the community. In both cases, what was involved was a mere repetition of outlines of thought and action, which gradually lost their meaning and became agents of alienation of the faithful. As Paul Ricoeur has pointed out, mechanical repetition of formulae rapidly becomes a *rhetoric of domination*, that is, the ideological justification of an established order. The only way of avoiding domination—and its rhetoric—in the transmission of faith, is to be found in *experience*, which is another name for the re-creation achieved on the basis of a *living community language*, one that can be *spoken* by each believer in his own way.[12]

3. THE EXPERIENCE AND SYMBOLISM OF TIME

(a) The crisis of community life

Bearing in mind that religion is a communicative activity in the bosom of the community tradition, the essential point is that man *speaks*. He does so in a sense full of possibilities, since man is always a potential *polyglot*, who *states* reality and at the same time *utters* himself to himself through the multiple expressive faculties at his command. 'Man, even in his present neo-capitalist and pseudo-socialist debased state, is a wonderful being because he—sometimes—speaks.'[13] Western official tradition, however, has led to a progressive muzzling of man's capacity for speech,[14] or rather to the virtually absolute primacy of one type of language (technical-economic) at the expense of others. Iconographic, narrative, aesthetic, allusive and other speech-forms have become irrelevant; we have forgotten their capacity to express *time*, which is not simply the 'useful' time of the 'time is money' school. In this sense, the lack of understanding shown by so many anthropologists of the last century, and even of this, is symptomatic: faced (even if often only through their reading) with what were patronisingly called 'savage' or 'primitive' peoples, Spencer, Morgan, Lubbock, Frazer *et al.* not only showed themselves firm pillars of 'colonialist ideology', but demonstrated their own lack of communicative ability, their dumbness in the face of the worlds of symbolism and religion they encountered. In this they decisively reduced the ambit of what is human, since only what he is capable of expressing exists for man. Hence the ravages of 'colonialist ideology' have not only been destructive in their acquiescence in the appropriation and exploitation of the human and natural resources of non-western peoples but also because they have plundered the *expressive riches* of these cultures, quarantining their valuable linguistic resources which enabled them to find their personal and community identity in their own *here and now*.

It has been said that 'for a society to serve as the common context for the life and action of individuals, there has to be a universal frame of reference . . . and this frame of reference has to be shared by at least most of the members of that society'.[15] Without this common framework of integration, the world ceases to be the setting in which we can find the overall meaning of existence. In pre-modern society, this framework was generally *religious*. 'For the individual, this meant simply that the *same* set of integrating symbols impregnated the different aspects of everyday life. In the family, at work, taking part in political activities or in feasts and ceremonies, the individual found himself always in the same "world".'[16] Modern society, on the other hand, is characterised by a plurality of environments which, at best, produce only a 'multi-relational synchronisation'.[17] Each individual, to safeguard his identity, tries to create 'his domestic world', in which 'the family functions as a workshop for life planning'.[18]

In such a situation, it would seem that the right to progress, expressed through the multiplicity of systems that make up modern society, is in competition with, and sometimes even in direct opposition to, the rights of tradition.[19] Faced with this new state of affairs, the greatest problem is not the abandonment of some traditional forms and institutions due to social change, but the creation of new traditions capable of guiding the lives of individuals and communities in a world in an accelerating process of change.[20] The loss of meaning attached to traditional religious modes has given rise to the 'privatisation of religion': a concept which, in the words of Antonio Marzal, 'is evident in the most negative sense of the term—the paleoliberal sense—as an infantile inferiority complex in the face of political speech which is uncritically assumed to be superior'.[21] But the privatisation of religion—and in the broader context, the 'decline of political man' (Sennet)—does not solve man's peremptory need to express his personal and community experience of reality as something many-faceted and harmonious. The understanding of man as '*chacun*' and '*aucun*' (M. de Certeau) imposes a retreat into the 'private sphere' if man is to achieve any 'personalisation', though it should be said that this is not the way to reach fulfilment of the human desire to 'live eternity in time' (M. Eliade).[22]

(b) Compelling symbolisation

The crisis of community life is particularly noticeable in man's loss of his symbolic capacity. Space and time are the two dimensions that delineate human existence. Both have suffered the negative effects of a rationalism which has forgotten that human space and time also possess sharply differentiated expressive modes. Here I am referring particularly to time, though *human history* is incomprehensible without *human geography*.

(i) Feasts

Here and there hopeful signs are emerging that *homo ludens* will once more be somehow taken account of in western culture. Modern anthropologists of human wishes (Castaneda, Bataille, Bastide, Desroche) have shown that any study of man limited to consideration of him as *homo faber* is bound to be incomplete and often grossly distorting. In practice, there is a return to festivity, to play-acting, to the 'change of level' (Eliade): there is a 'romanticisation of existence'.[23]

Space here prevents a detailed consideration of what is an authentic 'feast'. But what it is not is mere 'distraction', 'boredom' or a pause in the febrile activity of man dedicated to ever-greater productivity. 'Essentially the feast consists in tranquillity, as opposed to the greedy intranquillity of everyday life: a tranquillity which embraces intensity and contemplation, and can unite them when intensity reaches relaxation.'[24] So feasts are characterised by human encounters devoted not to greater work effort, but to feeling, intuiting the unity, fullness and beauty of reality, beyond the apparent chaos and distortion of the everyday. So the authentic feast exists on a plane beyond dogma and ethics, in the sphere of *gratuitousness* and *fullness of meaning*. Going beyond the language of prescription, the unsayable (Rilke) produces its Epiphany, thereby anticipating *in statu viae* the *status patriae* for those who truly celebrate the feast.

For nineteenth-century religion, 'work is prayer' (Carlyle). The original *ora et labora*, which supposed a creative tension between *homo ludens* and *homo faber*, has been reduced—first by 'bourgeois ideology' and later by 'technico-economic rationalism'—to an understanding of man oblivious of the fact that he possesses a congenital ability to symbolise and experience time both as *chronos* and as *kairos*. Tellenbach has made an apt summary of the reasons for the loss of man's festive sense as a result of theories of progress stemming from the Enlightenment: (1) the impoverishment of human actions; (2) the trivialisation of the rhythm of life, indispensable to the authentic feast; (3) the atrophy of the sense of the numinous; (4) the loss of conviction that life, the everyday pattern, can reach mystery, divinity.[25] This process has produced a 'crisis of differences' (R. Girard), which disclocate man, a relational being *par excellence*, both in relation to the 'world of history' and in relation to the *prius* and *supra* which condition his overall existence. The feast's 'consecration of the moment' constitutes precisely anticipation and experience of what man *is* and *will be*.[26]

(ii) Time experienced and symbolised

The feast is part of man's authentic existence, since in it he finds his temporality expressed in a different and complimentary way from, for example, 'the world of industrial relations'. Experience is the enriching passage through life; this passage is symbolised and realised in different directions, and consequently expressed in different languages. No expressive medium alone 'possesses a richness of vocabulary established once and for all and capable of communicating the needs of the spirit; words which originally denoted another experience of meaning or of everyday life are continually being borrowed'.[27] Every man and every community, living in their particular time and space, different from any other in their everyday pattern, should draw from the 'womb of memory' (St Augustine) representations of their common past and of the common future to which they are heading. 'The origins and goals of the community' do not consist in its *nunc stans*, but in experienced calling to mind, which is not to be confused with mere archaeology and anticipation of the end of history, which cannot be reduced to mere faultless planning of the future. This lies at the root of the only hope man has *at present* of symbolically anticipating the fullness of time. This task, which is both urgent and difficult, requires continual *re-creation* of man's relationships with himself, with his fellows, with nature and with God, and *deconstruction* of what is held to be normative and definitively institutionalised. On the way—in *ex-perientia*, whose best personal and community expression is the feast—man comes across the Epiphany of his humanity, which always means presence in the shape of absence, since Wish continues to be Wish. If they are to experience and symbolise time as not merely *chronos* in each new juncture, man and the community must of necessity reactivate their *grammar*. In effect: the *reform of language* as a continuous process is the indispensable condition for avoiding the reduction of the particularities of human spacio-temporal experience to an assemblage of approved words (orthodoxy) or a catalogue of norms (orthopraxis) poured out by the coercive presence of authority. Because reality—and mankind in it—is more than mere dogma and ethics: at every moment of personal and community existence expression must be given to *my* particular time, to *my* view of the world and of God.[28]

The *Deus semper maior*, who is in no way a *Deus alienus*, requires constant re-symbolisation in the midst of the hurly-burly of life of the *impression* made by his presence-absence on the consciousness of the individual, which impression is a foretaste *in statu viae* of the individual's *status patriae*.

4. CONCLUSION

Individual and collectives consciousness are always bound up in a particular history and tradition, which are expressed symbolically, in narrative form. This is how it is possible to actualise the affective and effective bonds which exist between members of the community. So Adorno writes that 'tradition is always immanent in any understanding as the mediating moment of its objects. One cannot pose any question which does not include transmission of past knowledge and conservation of knowledge for the future.' This community-constituting activity is not determined by a network of economic or political interests, but by what the poet José María Valverde has called 'the great angel of language'. The modern world is suffering a deep crisis of the word; its results are lack of communication and violence, and these will not be resolved through greater rationalisation and technocratisation of human relationships, since any historical *ratio* has its own preservation as a *sine qua non*. Only the rediscovery of the 'forgotten languages' which the value-added society had relegated to the domain of the insignificant in human terms, would enable us to experience once more that 'no idea of God can replace the myth of God'.[29] This myth of God, injected into daily life through memory, presence and anticipation, is not just a sentimental, nostalgic memory of paradise lost, but first and foremost the decided will to feel God in history and establish brotherhood among men. The common origin of all mankind indicates here and now the direction to be taken towards their common land. On this road, the stranger becomes a brother; the brother becomes humanity and destiny. The symbolisation of time requires discernment of spirit between 'own' and 'other'; a discernment inexorably requiring the 'other' to open out into what is 'common' to all mankind.

Translated by Paul Burns

Notes

1. R. Bastide 'Prométhée et son vautour. Essai sur la modernité et l'anti-modernité *Arch. Intern. Sociol. Coop.* 36 (1947) 6-21.
2. R. Dadoun 'Mais quel Occident? Quels autres' in *En marge. L'Occident et ses 'autres'* (Paris 1978) 11.
3. *Ibid.* 18-21.
4. E. Volant *Le Jeu des affranchis* (Montreal 1977).
5. See J.-P. Willaime 'Capitalisme et déstructuration symbolique' *Conf. Intern, Sociol. des Religions* XIV (Strasbourg 1977) 359-364; R. Sennet *The Fall of Public Man* (New York 1977); E. Biser *Theologische Sprachtheorie und Hermeneutik* (Munich 1970).
6. See Ll. Duch 'Coneixement científic i coneixement mític' *Qüestiones de Vida Cristiana* 82 (1976) 29-46.
7. On the two functions of religion, see Duch *Esperença cristiana i esforc humà* (Montserrat 1976) 54-70.
8. Duch 'Catequesi i llenguatge religiós' *Qüest. de. Vida Crist.* 89 (1977) 32-48.
9. See G. Balandier *Sens et puissance. Les dynamiques sociales* (Paris 1971).
10. *Ibid.* p. 289.
11. It is hardly necessary to point out that this cultural homogenisation is largely dominated by the selfish interests of the great powers, who have 'exported' their worries to the poor countries and imported primary produce and labour to augment their own well-being.
12. Duch 'Catequesi . . .', the article cited in note 8, 36-38.
13. O. Paz *Los signos en rotación y otros ensayos* (Madrid 1971) p. 164.
14. See W. Hartmann *Menschen in sprashloser Zeit. Zur Orientierung zwischen den Generationen* (Stuttgart 1973).
15. P. Berger *et al. The Homeless Mind* (New York 1973) p. 105.
16. *Idem.* p. 64.
17. *Idem.* p. 70.
18. Cf. *idem* pp. 67-69, 71.
19. See H. Lübbe *Fortschritt als Orientierungsproblem. Aufklärung in der Gegenwart* (Freiburg 1976) p. 32.
20. *Idem.* pp. 37, 55-56.
21. A. Marzal 'Una aproximació sociopolítica al fenomen de la privatització de la fe' *Qüest. de Vida. Crist.* 94 (1978) 41.
22. See Duch *De la religió a la religió popular. Religió entre il lustració i romanticisme* (Montserrat 1980) pp. 84-104.
23. See F. Benítez *En la tierra mágica del peyote* (Mexico[3] 1976), pp. 188-190.
24. K. Kerényi *Die antike Religion* (Düsseldorf-Cologne 1952).
25. See H. Tellenbach 'Zur Krise des Kultischen. Kilturpsychopathologische Erörterungen' *Anthropologie des Kults. Die Bedeutung des Kults für das Überleben des Menschen* (Freiburg-Basle-Vienna 1977) 87-93.
26. See Duch *De la religió* . . ., pp. 76-77.
27. H. Arendt *The Life of the Mind* (New York 1971).
28. See Ll. Duch *La experiencia religiosa en el contexto de la cultura comtemporánea* (Barcelona 1979) pp. 67-80.
29. R. Panikkar *Worship and Secular Man* (New York 1973). See this in conjunction with my 'Llenguatges oblidats en teologia' *Qüest. de Vida. Crist.* 93 (1978) 60-83.

PART II

Particular Questions

Anscar Chupungco

Liturgical Feasts and the Seasons of the Year

1. EASTER AND PENTECOST: SPRINGTIME AND HARVEST

IT IS an accepted fact that a number of liturgical feasts originated from or are associated with the seasons of the year and their festivals. Examples of such feasts are Easter and Pentecost, Christmas and Epiphany, Presentation of Our Lord, John the Baptist, Michael the Archangel and rogation and ember days.[1] The history and content of each feast reveal how in the formation of the liturgical calendar the Church took into account the various seasons of the year. Indeed certain cosmic elements and phenomena influenced the date of feasts and played a decisive role in the development of their themes and rituals. In the process of adapting the universal calendar to particular regions, especially outside the northern hemisphere, it is important to consider the nature of the relationship between the feast and the season: is the season a constitutive element of the date of the feast, or does it merely provide the feast with appropriate signs and symbols?

1. EASTER AND PENTECOST: SPRINGTIME AND HARVEST

In the case of Easter the Church adapted the Jewish feast of Passover and gave it a thoroughly Christian meaning. In the process of inculturation the elements of spring, equinox and full moon which together constitute the date of Passover were scrupulously retained. In fact the Quartodeciman controversy during the first two centuries was a debate on the theology of Easter based on the observance of the date of the Jewish Passover. Although Easter Sunday triumphed over Easter on 14 Nisan regardless of Sunday, the Church never abandoned spring equinox and the full moon in reckoning the date of Easter. Easter must fall during the *mensis novorum* when God, according to rabbinic tradition, created the world and led the Israelites out of Egypt, and when Christ, according to Christian tradition, celebrated his Passover from this world to the Father. Similarly the observance of the fifty days of Easter, which Irenaeus of Lyons claimed to have begun in apostolic times, corresponds to the Jewish harvest festival lasting for seven weeks. While the Jewish Pentecost ended with the renewal of the covenant (2 Chron. 15:10-14), Christian Pentecost ended with the bestowal of the Holy Spirit.[2]

Clearly the early Church, in assuming Jewish festivals and imbuing them with

31

Christian meaning, respected their seasonal character. The patristic Easter tracts and homilies are difficult to appreciate, if they are not read in the context of spring, equinox and full moon. Indeed these cosmic elements project the paschal themes of creation, rebirth, light and presence of salvation. While the mystery of human salvation is brought about by the death and resurrection of Christ and shared by the Church through the paschal sacraments, it is ushered in by the season which alone eloquently portrays it. There is, therefore, something more than mere symbolism in the date of Easter: it is the agent which brings about the yearly presence of paschal salvation. However, one cannot overlook the fact that spring possesses certain signs and symbols which had an influence on the development of paschal theology. In other words, the season of spring with its equinox and full moon constitutes the Easter date. At the same time it provides the feast with rich theology whose language is truly experiential. But an intriguing question is whether spring is first of all a date and only secondly a symbol. If it is first and foremost the historical date of Christ's death and resurrection, then Easter as an anniversary has to be celebrated during spring in the northern hemisphere which is summer in the equator and autumn in the southern hemisphere. But if spring is primarily symbolic, Easter is more meaningful during the spring of the southern hemisphere and the season closest to spring in the equatorial regions.

It may be useful to recall that the liturgical calendar is luni-solar. Some feasts, especially the 'birthdays' of saints, follow the fixed date of the solar calendar. Easter on the other hand has a movable date conditioned by the full moon of the vernal equinox. Easter date is therefore constituted by cosmic elements which are not tied to one particular solar date. The point of the matter is that the date of Easter which is not solar according to our calendar but lunar according to the course of the seasons is truly a date to which the historical event of Christ's death and resurrection has always been assigned by tradition. Since Easter is an anniversary or an annual anamnesis of the paschal mystery, it should somehow coincide with the historical date, otherwise Easter will be reduced to an ordinary Sunday anamnesis and the yearly cycle of feasts will be confused with the weekly. Since, according to tradition, the historical date corresponded to the season of spring in the northern hemisphere, what matters in the final analysis is not the season of spring, but the equivalent calendar date that defines the historical date, regardless of the season during which it occurs in the other hemispheres.[3] After all, no one would consider celebrating an anniversary on a date far-removed from the historical event.

Obviously preference for the date will minimise the symbolic role played by spring, equinox and full moon. As Eusebius of Caesarea notes, no other season of the year is appropriate for Easter celebration; for in winter nature is melancholic, in summer it is burnt by the sun, and in autumn it is bereft and despoiled of its fruit.[4] Easter in the equator falls during the summer months, and in the southern hemisphere, during autumn. In both cases the symbolism of rebirth and new life is ostentatiously absent. One will have to play up the theological message of the feast to cover up the season's contradiction. However, a better approach to the problem is the creation of language and symbols derived from summer or autumn. It was certainly easier for the Fathers of the Church to indulge slavishly in spring symbols, to relate the rebirth of man in baptism with the rebirth of nature in spring, to perceive the special presence of God, Creator and Saviour, in the *epidemia* of the season. But this should not halt symbolic creativity in the liturgy. Perhaps awed by the grandeur of patristic heritage, we have become more concerned with its preservation than with the imitation of what the Fathers have done in the past and would have done today. Summer and autumn, like springtime, are also *kairoi*, that is, seasons of God's presence among men. Is it not possible that they should also be able to offer the feast of feasts the homage of a new language and new symbols which can also eloquently and graphically express the message of Easter?

2. CHRISTMAS AND EPIPHANY: WINTER SOLSTICE AND BIRTH OF LIGHT

The feasts of Christmas and Epiphany present a dimension quite different from that of Easter. Here one may not speak of a historical date, but of a seasonal festival. Although they fall on different dates, they have basically the same content: manifestation, apparition and advent of Christ, the light of the world.[5] The Roman winter solstice on 25 December and the Egyptian on 6 January marked the appearance of the sun which triumphed over the darkness of winter. From then on the days would be longer and the nights shorter. It is not surprising that already in the second century the gnostic sect of Basilides commemorated the baptism of Jesus on 6 January; for the sect believed that the incarnation, and hence the apparition, of the Word took place at the Jordan. Neither is it surprising that by the fourth century Rome assumed the Mithraic *natalis solis invicti* and by process of inculturation transformed it into the birthday of Christ, his appearance in human flesh. Thus at the turn of the year at mid-winter the early Church celebrated her own *rites de passage* from darkness to light, as she welcomed the appearance of the true light of the world.[6]

Unlike the date of Easter, the dates of Christmas and Epiphany have no historical basis. Hence, there should be no difficulty, historically and theologically speaking, in moving the date of Christmas to the mid-winter of the southern hemisphere or its equivalent in the equator. The problem is rather of a practical nature. At this stage it would seem too late to change a date which is universally accepted, even in non-Christian countries. To move it to another date for the sake of a more vivid symbolism may not be worth the trouble, considering how it would upset an international date.

What is worth the trouble is the creation of symbols derived from the season during which Christmas falls. It should be recalled that the central message of the feast is the manifestation of light, man's victory over darkness, and the dawn of salvation in Christ. Cold winter nights and snow (or white cotton placed on Christmas trees to feign snow!) are not symbolic or representative of Christmas. Christmas means sun, radiant light, turning-point of winter gloom. That Christmas falls during the summer months of the southern hemisphere may after all not be so lamentable. The language of the liturgy too should consider the particular seasonal phenomena, following the tradition of liturgical hymnology which commemorates God's creation, times and seasons of the year. In this way the liturgy can eliminate the contradiction between songs about 'the cold winter night' of Christmas and the reality of a scorching summer sun.

3. OTHER FEASTS: OTHER SEASONAL TURNING-POINTS

Other feasts, like the Presentation of Our Lord, John the Baptist and Michael the Archangel, suggest a close association with seasonal festivals, if not a direct derivation. The Presentation of Our Lord, for example, which was fixed on 2 February by Emperor Justinian in 542, need not be regarded as an adaptation of an oriental pagan festival of lights or torches observed on 1 February to welcome the return of the divinity from the underworld.[7] At any rate the feast was celebrated by the middle of the fourth century in Jerusalem, forty days after Epiphany, with a procession to the Anastasis. Etheria speaks of a procession, but is silent about the use of candles, which was introduced only a century later.[8] Although Luke 2:32 seems to have directly inspired the procession with lights, one cannot dismiss the possible influence of a seasonal festival, however far it may lay at the background. For purposes of adaptation, it may be noted here that this feast, which in biblical arrangement took place forty days after the birth of Jesus, is dependent on the date of Christmas and shares its theme of light.

A feast of strongly cosmic or seasonal character is the Birthday of John the Baptist which has been observed by the western Church on 24 June since the beginning of the fifth century. That the Roman calendar assigned it in June, six months before Christmas, can be understood in the light of Luke 1:36; but that it assigned the feast precisely on 24 June indicates a certain purpose. In one of his homilies on the Birthday of John the Baptist Augustine explains: 'Today John is born: from today on the days become shorter; on 25 December Christ was born: from that day on the days become longer.'[9] Augustine's explanation concurs with John's saying: 'He must increase, and I must decrease.' (John 3:30). But it also harmonises with the cosmic phenomenon of summer solstice, when the sun retraces its course and gives in to autumn and winter. In ancient civilisation summer solstice was a critical turning-point in the solar course, for it announced the death of nature. Probably to reinforce the weakening power of the sun as it glided down its winter course, fire festivals and torch processions were held. The middle ages continued this tradition, reinterpreting it in the context of John the Baptist, by lighting the midsummer fires on mountains and hills.[10] Thus the Church sanctified an important turning-point of the annual solar course by incorporating it into the Christian mystery.

Not only spring equinox, winter solstice and summer solstice, but also autumnal equinox received special liturgical consideration. The Sacramentary of Verona offers as many as five formularies for the dedication of the basilica of Michael the Archangel at the Salarian Way.[11] The date given by the Sacramentary is 30 September, that is, after the autumnal equinox, when the sun decidedly enters its downward course and leaves the world dead and cold. At such a critical moment the Church invokes the protection of the great champion against evil forces. It is interesting to note that in pre-Christian Rome there was a custom of assigning at this season a *dictator* with extraordinary authority, who entered into his office by fixing a nail on the right-side wall of the temple of Jupiter on the Capitoline hill. The fixed nail symbolised a stop to human illness and natural disaster occasioned by the change of seasons. The dictator himself was regarded as a general protector of the city.[12]

With the feast of Michael the Archangel all four cardinal points of the year are assumed into the liturgy. Indeed they become *kairoi*, that is, sacred times when the Church intensely experiences the saving presence of God. It should be remembered that man, who has always been profoundly sensitive to the critical moments of seasonal changes, created festivals or *rites de passage* to welcome God's blessings or escape the calamities caused by such changes. It should also be recalled that rabbinic tradition assigned festivals recalling the history of salvation at the cardinal points of the year. Thus at the equinox of spring God created the world and led his people out of Egypt. The principal events of history were commemorated at the principal turning-points of the year. No wonder then that the Church filled the four seasons with feasts that helped her children to face the forces of nature with confidence. The choice of feasts was done at random and with complete freedom. Easter date comes from the Jewish tradition, Christmas from a Roman festival, John the Baptist and Michael the Archangel from seasonal turning-points. However, there is a certain logic in the choice. If Easter means rebirth and new life, spring is the most appropriate season; if Christmas indicates the dawn of salvation, winter solstice is obviously the date to celebrate it; if John the Baptist is the herald of a new age and the end of the old, summer solstice is the adequate moment to keep his birthday; and if Michael the Archangel is the protector of the Church, he is rightly invoked at the autumnal equinox.

These considerations have a practical bearing on the adaptation of the liturgical calendar to other cultures and regions outside the northern hemisphere. Even in the industrial world man is affected by the changes of seasons. And in regions where the only change is between dry and wet, one cannot remain unimpressed by either the mildness or the violence of nature. It is within this seasonal framework that the Church can, with the probable exception of the date of Easter, reconsider her seasonal feasts. For if in the case of the sanctoral the liturgy has traditionally observed the concurrence of the feast with the 'birthday' of the saint, with greater reason should it take into account the seasons of the year and the various seasonal festivals and rites existing in different regions of the world.

4. ROGATION AND EMBER DAYS: THE CYCLE OF HUMAN WORK

According to the General Norms on the Liturgical Year, no. 45: 'On rogation and ember days the Church publicly thanks the Lord and prays to him for the needs of men, especially for the productivity of the earth and for man's labour.' Because of the agricultural origin of these days the Church urges the Conferences of Bishops to adapt their date and celebration to the situations obtaining in the region. Thus both rogation and ember days should reflect the actual needs of the working man and the agricultural conditions of each place.

A brief historical sketch of these days may be useful to the work of adapting the liturgical calendar not only to the seasons but also to other human work besides the agricultural. The rogation days before Ascension, for example, had no agricultural association. They were litanies chanted during solemn outdoor processions instituted by the Bishop of Vienne in 470 to invoke God's protection during earthquakes. Rogation days therefore can be held for various human needs, especially those involving the community. But it is the major rogation day traditionally held on 25 April that originated from the agricultural world. On this day ancient Rome held the Robigalia, a feast in honour of the god or goddess Robigo whom farmers invoked to preserve the crops from red mildew. They held a procession to the grove of Robigo by the Claudian Way and there offered sacrifices to the divinity. In the sixth century Christians still kept the same route, except that the procession ended at the Vatican.[13] These details show how the Church assumed the agricultural ritual of a society, purified it and elevated it to the status of a Christian celebration. Whether Gregory the Great ordered its observance in order to counteract the pagan rite or show the Church's respect for the farmers' tradition is difficult to ascertain. What is important to note is that the Church was genuinely sensitive to the needs of the working man; especially at those moments when the forces of nature threatened the fruit of his labour. It is at times like this that the liturgy can be a meaningful expression of men's confidence in divine protection and of their solidarity in times of adversity.

While rogation days centred on litanies and processions, ember days stressed prayer, fasting and alms-giving. Pope Leo the Great mentions the practice of fasting in spring, summer, autumn and winter; and the liturgy readily sets it against the background of Old Testament observance.[14] But in reality ember days were the Christian counterpart of the Roman festivals at seed-time, grain harvest and vintage, which were held respectively in the months of November-December, June-August and September-October.[15] Instead of the external festivities which marked the pagan festivals, the Church by contrast chose to pass these critical seasonal changes in prayer, fasting and good works. This does not mean that the Church ignored the agricultural overtones of these days. The ember days of Pentecost and September, for example, retained a notable link with the offering of the first grain harvest and vintage.

In adapting ember days to local situations it is useful to underline the communitarian character of these observances. The Church, during these days, appealed to the Christians as a community, as a people who stand in need of God's aid and are grateful for favours received. It is also useful to stress that the observance of ember days should harmonise with the spirit of the liturgical seasons. Fasting and other penitential practices, for example, have no place in the Easter season; on the other hand, good works in terms of social concern are appropriate during Lent. Lastly, local traditions connected with the seasons, like the offering and blessing of first fruits, should be preserved, if possible, and imbued with liturgical meaning. Thus, the observance of ember days will not be merely ascetical and penitential but also properly liturgical.

5. CONCLUSION

The historical approach to the question of liturgical feasts and the seasons of the year does not offer instant solutions to the problem of adaptation. On the contrary, it demands a careful and serious research into the meaning of the Christian feasts and the connaturality of seasons and their festivals to serve as vehicles of the Christian mystery. Adaptation, in this particular case, implies a respect for the structure and rationale of the liturgical year as the unfolding of the whole mystery of Christ in the course of the entire year. The pastoral aspect of adaptation, therefore, revolves around the problem of communicating the mystery of Christ to the faithful, in such a way that they are enabled to lay hold of it, to experience it, and to celebrate it within the framework of the natural order. And while it may prove useful to move the date of certain feasts to the appropriate seasons, it is not only an ideal but also an urgent need to adapt and create new liturgical language and symbols based on the seasons of the year.

Notes

1. E. O. James *Seasonal Feasts and Festivals* (New York 1965) pp. 199-238.
2. N. Denis-Boulet *Le Calendrier chrétien* (Paris 1959) pp. 20-25; T. Maertens *A Feast in Honour of Yahweh* (London 1967) pp. 98-151; H.-J. Kraus *Worship in Israel* (Oxford 1966) pp. 45-61; J. Van Goudoever *Biblical Calendars* (Leiden 1961) pp. 182-194.
3. A. Chupungco *The Cosmic Elements of Christian Passover* (Rome 1977) pp. 105-114.
4. PG 24, 696C. See: *Homélies pascales I* Sources Chrétiennes 27 (1959) p. 145; Gaudentius of Brescia *Tractatus I in Exodum* CSEL LXVIII (1936) p. 18.
5. P. Jounel 'Le temps de Noël' *L'Eglise en Prière* (Paris 1961) pp. 727-738.
6. B. Botte *Les origines de la Noël et de l'Epiphanie* (Louvain 1932) pp. 68-76; H. Rahner *Greek Myths and Christian Mystery* (London 1963) pp. 134-157.
7. Pagan Rome celebrated during the first week of February a procession called *amburbium*, which J. Jungmann suspects to be the origin of the procession on 2 February. See: N. Turchi *La religione de Roma antica* (Bologna 1939) p. 121; J. Jungmann *The Early Liturgy* (London 1966) pp. 145-146.
8. *Journal de Voyage* Sources chrétiennes 21 (1971) p. 207; see: E. O. James in the book cited in note 1, at pp. 232-234.
9. *Sermo 287*, PL 38, 1302.
10. E. O. James, in the book cited in note 1, at p. 226.
11. *Sacramentarium Veronense* Rerum Ecclesiasticarum Documenta Fontes I (1978) nn. 844-869.
12. N. Turchi, in the work cited in note 7, at pp. 98-99.
13. *Ibid.* p. 85; J. Jungmann, in the book cited in note 7, at p. 145.
14. *Sermo 19, 2*, PL 54, 186.
15. A. Chavasse 'Les quatre-temps' *L'Eglise en Prière*, cited in note 5, at pp. 737-746.

Irénée-Henri Dalmais

At One Time and in One Place: Local Calendars and their Promotion

1. COSMIC GROUNDING

THERE IS only one Christian feast pure and simple: the celebration of the Lord's Pasch. Its annual commemoration began very early—from at least the first half of the second century—among all Christian communities, though complete agreement has never been reached even to this day, in spite of numerous and forceful admonitions, on the exact date at which it should be set. The serious disagreements regarding the question of Easter which arose during the second half of the second century, and which concerned the very meaning of the celebration, are well known. It is also well known that the seemingly exact rules laid down at the Council of Nicaea soon proved impracticable because of differences regarding the complex process of computation. The Gregorian calendar reform of 1582 started a new divergence of the practice of the churches of the western tradition from those of the eastern tradition; this problem is still unresolved.[1]

Nevertheless these disagreements had to do only with the precise dating of the feast, in regard to the principle of double reference to the full moon following the vernal equinox and to the Sunday after the Jewish celebration of the *Pessah*, in order to avoid a coincidence which might have caused problems in certain circles. The present difficult adjustments made in order to fix the date more precisely so that it is more appropriate to modern society as well as common to all, do at least preserve the principle of Sunday celebration and the relation with the vernal equinox. They ignore, however, the lunar cycle and therefore weaken the connections between the Christian Easter and the Jewish Pasch in which it is rooted and to which it must always refer. Moreover, the loss of any association with the lunar cycle can hardly be a matter of indifference to all those cultures which use it as a system of reference. Hence the reservations expressed about these proposals are wholly understandable. Above all there are the problems encountered in any attempt to establish a universally appropriate calendar. Finally, the connotations of the Easter celebration are attenuated in all those areas where it does not coincide with the springtime awakening of nature to which the liturgical texts so often allude and which made it possible to integrate with the Christian commemoration a number of popular practices handed down from a distant past. It is widely

37

acknowledged that the theme of Easter as the beginning of a new creation was reflected by kindred vernal images and notions from the Mediterranean world to the forests of Germany and Russia. Clearly the Christian celebration of the mystery of salvation could not ignore its cosmic grounding, even though that aspect would not be deemed essential.[2] Moreover, what I have just said of Easter applies to the entire cycle which developed quite early on, as regards both the weeks of quadragesimal preparation and the Pentecostal culmination grafted onto the ancient Jewish harvest festival.

Reference to cosmic cycles plays a secondary rôle in the establishment of a date for the celebration of Easter and of all the liturgical developments to which it gave rise; somewhat different, however, is the case of all those feasts and commemorations which for centuries have occupied a more or less major place in the various Christian calendars. One pole in particular was established fairly soon, and centred upon the theme of the 'manifestation' or Epiphany of Christ; it was constituted more especially with the commemoration of that first manifestation of Christ which represents his birth in the flesh. The origins and forms of expression of this focal point were complex; hence it was from the start associated with very widely distributed festivities marking the period of the winter solstice. The celebration of the Epiphany, centred upon a commemoration of the baptism which inaugurated Jesus' Messianic mission, most probably originated in the complex of festivals known to have been celebrated in Egypt in the month of Tybi—which more or less corresponds to our January.[3] But it was also associated at a very early date with the solar cycle and the first discernible signs of lengthening days. We may take it as accepted (in spite of all the efforts to associate it with the historical date of Jesus' birth) that the establishment of this *natale* is to be sought in Rome, more exactly perhaps on the Vatican hill, the place set apart for the celebration on the VIII Calends of January (25 December) of the *natalis solis invicti* which since Aurelius had been one of the high-points of the Imperial religion. Obviously this date was chosen because it was so close to the winter solstice. Hence two of the major feasts accepted in all Christian calendars[4] owe their date and even their origin to local situations, and undoubtedly to the wish to give a Christian meaning to festivals to which the people were still deeply attached. The association of these feasts with a cosmic cycle which was identical for the entire northern hemisphere must have influenced their popular acceptance. In addition, the Christianisation of areas more to the south than those which had produced them enhanced the feasts with new associations which, in their turn, were carried onwards by missionaries to regions where they were hardly meaningful.

Moreover, a considerable complex of feasts, deemed commemorative of events in the life of Christ or his mother and of facts reported in the gospels, gradually entered the liturgical calendars. The most significant case in this regard is the celebration on 25 March, very close to the spring equinox, of the annunciation to Mary of the incarnation of the Word of God. In its turn this celebration led to the establishment three months later, on 21 June (that is, in direct association with the summer solstice), of the *natale* according to the flesh of John the Forerunner. Finally a special place must be given, in the same perspective, to the Feast of the Presentation of Jesus in the Temple, forty days after his birth (2 February). This celebration appeared in Jerusalem very early on; Etheria witnessed it as already a most solemn commemoration on the fortieth day of Epiphany (14 February) with a procession through the church of the Anastasis. It was only at the end of the sixth century, when Jerusalem accepted the commemoration of the *Natale Domini* on 25 December, not 6 January, that the celebration of the *Hypapante* ('meeting', i.e., Candlemas) was set as everywhere else on 2 February. But at Rome the procession with lighted candles took on a penitential character in protest against the ancient Roman procession of the Amburbalia; this specific feature was so emphatic that it could take place independently if the feast coincided with a (privileged)

Sunday. It is significant that the feast itself came most usually to be called the Purification—in relation, so it would seem, to the former purification rites which marked the month of February and from which the name derived. Here, too, popular customs, such as that of eating special cakes, persisted apart from the feast when the exact signification had been forgotten.

Whatever the original grounding (and the influence which might as a result have been exerted by traditions and local customs whose meaning more or less disappeared, as the specifically Christian significance became established such celebrations with a direct reference to the manifestation in Christ of the mystery of salvation could be accepted everywhere, and could appear a common basis for the liturgical calendars of the various Christian churches. Nevertheless, we must remember that it was only in the Latin West, and above all in the Roman tradition, that the fixed-date feasts of the mysteries of the Lord's life were integrated alongside the Easter celebrations into what has been called the 'temporal cycle'.

From the very time when an attempt was made to establish a liturgical calendar, the problem arose of trying to bring the lunar-solar computation which formed the basis of the organisation of the paschal cycle into line with the framework of the solar year which, from the Julian reform of 45 B.C., was accepted as the foundation of most of the calendars used in the Roman Empire. The increasingly dominant position of solar symbolism in the imperial religion and its transference into a Christian perspective were to ensure the definitive adoption in the Christian world of a liturgical calendar organised within the framework of the solar year. This meant a break with the Jewish tradition of a lunar-solar calendar and of course with all those calendars based only on the lunar cycle. But, until our own era at least, respect for the arrangement of the paschal cycle in accordance with Jewish tradition prevented a unified and fully harmonious organisation of the Christian liturgical calendar. The most determined effort was that made by the Syriac-Oriental Church of Mesopotamia and attributed to Catholicos Isho'yab III (+ 657).[5] It divided the whole year in accordance with a Pentecostal basis of seven weeks and a day for which the period of the forty days of Easter is the ideal type, the others being more or less complete. With rare exceptions, the various commemorations are allocated in accordance not with the day of the month but with the days of the various weeks. The Armenian liturgical year would seem to be organised in accordance with a similar pattern, as would that of the western Syrians of the Antiochian tradition—though in this instance the form is less rigorous.

2. ANNIVERSARIES

I shall leave aside the very characteristic case of the Coptic Church, which remained loyal to the old Egyptian calendar of the Roman era with its months of thirty days to which were added the five or six supplementary 'epagomenous' days, and its rhythm of three agricultural seasons of flood, seedtime and harvest. Everywhere else the reformed Roman calendar was imposed and the various Christian festal anniversaries and commemorations have been situated within its framework. For many centuries anniversaries of three types would seem to have prevailed for the most part.

The oldest and most usual types of anniversary are the *natalia*: that is, anniversaries ranging from the authentic birth to the definitive life in paradise of witnesses to the faith: martyrs, confessors, and pastors whose teaching and guidance strengthened the Church which had commissioned them. Such commemorations had a primarily local basis and were rooted in the age-old tradition of assemblies at a venerated tomb. Very soon, however, the fame of some of these witnesses led other churches to invoke their intercession and to celebrate their memory. Even then this cult would retain local

D

traces, and the commemoration would take place by preference in sanctuaries which held some material keepsake of the person venerated: oil or dust collected on the tomb, or some object (*brandea*) which had been left there. Later, when the strict Roman law regarding the inviolability of tombs had been attenuated, it would be some fragment of the individual's mortal remains (relics). Hence the basically local nature of the commemorative calendar was soon extended, especially because of the spread of major ecclesiastical centres. This was above all the case—though in a very different way—for Rome and Constantinople. On the other hand, those churches which remained enclosed within the framework of their specific traditions had hardly any room for commemorations of foreign origin. Though Coptic Egypt drew on its own resources for almost daily commemorations, it is important to stress that it was mainly within the setting of the local pilgrimage (*moulad*) that these assumed the nature of a liturgical and festal celebration. Besides, as I have already said, with few exceptions they took place not on the fixed date of an anniversary but on a specific day of the week close to that anniversary. From the middle of the fourth century (354) the Church of Rome drew up a list showing the place and date on which the anniversary of the *Depositio martyrum* was to be commemorated. This already includes a few African martyrs but also on 25 December the 'birth of Christ in Bethlehem of Judaea', and on 22 February—the traditional commemoration of the ancestors—it mentions the *Cathedra Petri*, with a reference to the accepted term for this commemoration which was honoured by each *gens*. The allocation of the places and dates of these commemorations has been thought to indicate a pastoral strategy in regard both to popular assemblies of the Christian community during the summer months and to evangelisation of the suburbs and outlying areas of the city.[6] It should be noted, too, that this local emphasis of the Roman commemorations lasted until the beginning of the thirteenth century.[7] But the case of Rome, the city of the apostles and martyrs, is exceptional. In the West there came into being, at least from the end of the sixth century (the *Auxerre recension* of 592) a calendar which amalgamated with the basic Roman version a list of African origin, and the more ecumenical calendar established at Nicomedia around 393.[8] The latter would seem to have been the first basis of the liturgical calendar of Constantinople, whose history is as yet undetermined.

The New Rome was unable to prevail, like the Old Rome, as the city of many martyrs, but it became concerned very early on to obtain relics and build *Martyria* for them. Sanctuaries were dedicated in honour of saints, of the mother of God or of one of the mysteries of the life of Christ. The importance of such dedications in the construction of Christian calendars grew continually. The oldest of which we are certain is that of the dedication of the Constantinian sanctuaries of the Martyrium and the Anastasis at Jerusalem on 13 September 335. Outside the Holy City this anniversary was replaced by that of the solemn Exaltation of the Cross on the second day of the Encenies (14 September). It is arguable that the dates chosen for the commemoration of the saints of the Old Testament, or for the apostles, for certain Marian feasts and so on, originated with the anniversary of the dedication of a local sanctuary whose prestige spread far and wide because of its fame or the status of the city in which it was built. Obviously such commemorations might also refer to the anniversary of the translation of some venerated relic. In both cases there was originally a local celebration whose primary reason was gradually obscured.

Finally, a number of celebrations were first established in order to commemorate the memory of an event which people wished to keep, whether it was an historical anniversary—a victory, a liberation or, on the contrary, the recollection of a serious crisis when it was thought that some supernatural intervention had been made—or a reference intended to give a Christian significance to some traditional commemoration. Perhaps we may include among feasts of this type those such as the Transfiguration of

Christ at the beginning of August, accepted late into the Roman liturgy in 1457 at the time when Rome learnt of the victory the previous year over the Turks—but its origin is much earlier; perhaps it was in a tradition of the Church of Jerusalem which would have provided a theme for Christianisation of the Armenian summer celebration at Vardavar (the rose). Such instances are not exceptional in the various calendars and testify to the insertion of the Christian liturgy into the framework of commemorations whose memory it was hoped to maintain by means of a new significance. As examples of seasonal feasts, I shall mention only the two Marian celebrations of the Syrian liturgies for sowing and harvest: Our Lady of Seedtime and Our Lady of the Grain. Symbolism of the same type allowed the integration in various ways of a liturgical blessing of the grapes during August, whether—among the Armenians—for the Feast of the Dormition of our Lady or—at Rome—in association with the commemoration of St Sixtus which was then within the framework of the Feast of the Transfiguration. It would be very interesting to gather examples of this procedure from the various local calendars. They indicate a general and constant interest in bringing Christian celebrations up to date and place. It is essential that the procedures should not be too arbitrary, as happened in a more recent era, especially in the Roman liturgy—one need think only of the solemnisation by Pius IX, on 1 July, of a Feast of the Precious Blood of Christ in thanksgiving for his return to Rome after a halt had been called to revolutionary agitation; or, more recently still, of the choice of St Joseph the Workman for a liturgical celebration on 1 May.

3. UNIVERSAL AND SPECIAL CALENDARS

In fact, in the Byzantine and in the Roman liturgies, the local nature of the organisation of the calendar was increasingly lost sight of, as the scale of its adoption and adaptation continued to grow. This goes a long way back in the case of Rome for, as I have said, the liturgical calendar of the City was supplemented from the Gallo-Frankish nations; from the end of the sixth century, by commemorations from Africa and from the eastern Christian world; then by numerous initially local or regional commemorations. Indeed they gave rise to a considerable number of the liturgical texts which gradually entered the Roman calendar towards the end of the twelfth century, only to be codified by the curial *ceremonarii* in the first half of the thirteenth century. The establishment in the same era of the mendicant orders—set apart from any local ties and using as the basis of their liturgy this new type of calendar—was to contribute greatly to its generalised use, and the addition of popular devotional commemorations. It was then that the Latin West began to speak of the *universal calendar*, and that the popes, the supreme governors of the religious orders, enthusiastically introduced new commemorations without any attempt at consistency. The renewal of the Roman liturgy decided on at the Council of Trent tried to bring some order into this chaos, and at the very least to suppress whatever seemed inadequately based or touched by superstition. But constantly renewed pressures soon stopped these initiatives, and the liturgical unification of the nineteenth century together with the extension of the missions helped this calendar to prevail on an increasingly universal scale.

A similar phenomenon occurred in the Byzantine liturgical year whose arrangements, with some modifications and several additions, were adopted by the churches of the Orthodox communion. The tendency was even encouraged because no authorised revision was undertaken, and the present state of affairs (whose history would not appear to have been researched) results mainly from the diffusion of printed texts whose origin and value remain uncertain.

The new 'general Roman calendar' promulgated by Pope Paul VI as of 14 February 1969 in fact represents an unprecedented innovation. The apostolic letter, or *motu proprio*, which approves it, from its opening words locates the whole order in the perspective of the celebration of the eastern mystery, with reference to directives established by the Vatican II Constitution on the Liturgy (chapter 5). The norms concerning the arrangement of the calendar show that it 'is general or local, depending on whether it is established for the use of the entire Roman rite, or for the use of a particular church or a religious order' (art. 48). Hence, on the one hand, this new calendar concerns only the churches of the Roman acceptation and, on the other hand, it explicitly provides for the establishment of special calendars for which directives were given on 24 June 1970 in the form of an instruction emanating from the Roman Congregation for Sacred Rites. In the present state of legislation only the churches known as the Churches of the Eastern Rite retain, within the Roman Catholic communion, the former order of their calendar. The norms approved *motu proprio* by apostolic letter of 14 February 1969 are offered as 'universal norms' for the liturgical year and for the new general Roman calendar. In fact the directive issued for the production of special calendars allows only minimal latitude for seemingly appropriate adaptations. Indeed, the general calendar shows that care has been taken to make obligatory only those commemorations which have become part of the pious practice of Catholic communities (on condition that they offer evidence of a definite historical foundation), with the sole addition of commemorations of representatives of various areas of the world or of the main religious orders. Such provisions are obviously inimical to any arrangement of the existing calendar in terms of local situations. The predominantly historical concern and the intention to locate saints' commemorations as far as possible on the actual anniversaries of their deaths has obscured the fact that some old dates were included in the seasonal calendar, and that a certain number of those were chosen originally in order to Christianise a traditional commemoration. Hence the new Roman calendar seems to abstract a construction without any authentic roots in real human circumstances. But that is surely the price which has to be paid for a calendar pretending to universal status. It is to be hoped that this process will result in greater diversification in terms of particular places and traditions. Experience shows that the rhythms of human life depend but minimally on authoritarian decisions and are governed by complex factors which authority should acknowledge and, if necessary, ratify rather than try to ordain.

Translated by John Cumming

Notes

1. See among the many works on the date of Easter: Vitterio Peri *The Date of Easter* (Vatican City 1968).
2. See Anscar J. Chupungco OSB *The Cosmic Elements of Christian Passover* (Rome 1977).
3. I.-H. Dalmais 'The Celebration of the Christmas Cycle in the Eastern churches' *Concilium* 102, 15-24; R. G. Coquin 'Les origines de l' Epiphanie en Egypt' *Noël, Epiphanie, Retour du Christ* (Paris 1967) 139-170.
4. With the exception only of the Armenians who have retained a single celebration on 6 January in accordance with the primitive Jerusalem usage.
5. According to H. and J. Lewy of Union College, Cincinnati (*Annual*, 1943, pp. 41-101), this arrangement of the calendar derives from the Sumerians and the Akkadians (cf see J. Mateos *Lelya-Sapra* (Rome 1973) p. 461, n. 2).
6. I.-H. Dalmais 'Etude sur le sanctoral romain' in *La Maison Dieu* 133 (1978) 106-107, with reference to C. Pietri *Roma christiana* (Rome 1976) pp. 127-129 and 365-366.
7. P. Jounel *Le Culte des saints dans les basiliques du Latran et du Vatican au douzieme siècle* (Rome 1977).
8. See P. Jounel 'Le Culte des saints' A. G. Martimort *L'Eglise en prière*, part IV, ch. 5 (Paris 1965).

Peter Eicher

The Age of Freedom:
A Christian Community for Leisure
and the World of Work

'Days and times should not control Christians. Rather, Christians freely exercise control over days and times.'

MARTIN LUTHER

TIME IS MONEY. In bourgeois industrial civilisation work is undertaken in order to acquire wages and to increase the money at one's disposal; leisure is devoted to the consumption of the goods obtained with money and to the pursuit of the cultural values obtained with money. Work and leisure emerge as simply two aspects of the single fundamental rhythm of the industrial age in general: the continually accelerating traffic in goods. This productive cycle that ultimately serves the consumption of the 'haves' was very precisely labelled by Karl Marx 'the religion of everyday life'.[1] The Christian community does not stand outside this social reality that is continually coming into being. Rather, within this closed universe of work and leisure it must decide whether it is going to go on sanctioning this religion of everyday life by providing a regular Sunday service of worship or whether in Christ Jesus it will try, by means of a new way of living as a community, to make ring out loud and clear the message of redeeming liberation from the domination of a world of production that has become all-powerful. Any practical theology that is concerned merely with an amelioration of the pastoral opportunities for week-ends and for the holiday industry and fails to see through the dominant ideologies of leisure, any practical theology that merely proposes improvements without a theoretical framework of the history of society and without the critical theology that goes with it—any practical theology on these lines will be unable to provide the Christian community with that service which is demanded of it precisely as theology. And what is demanded of theology is that it should take the message of God's action that is proclaimed in the Old and New Testaments and express it within and to our socially conditioned history in such a way that it can still be experienced and lived in its liberating power of redemption today. But because the 'life', the 'salvation', the 'redemption', the 'reconciliation' and the 'consummation' that God has wrought in his actual dealings with Israel and in Jesus Christ are not things that can be produced by work, created by society and organised politically, the Christian community which does not intend to serve the glorification of society's self-fulfilment comes into the strongest opposition to the bourgeois system of efficient achievement in its process of reproduction organised on the basis of private and State capital. But in the overdeveloped regions of this economically increasingly interdependent world, as well as in the regions they have kept underdeveloped, the Christian community can only enter into this liberating opposition to industrialised interaction if it allows itself to be fundamentally reformed by the spirit of Jesus Christ, who 'has set us free for freedom' (Gal. 5:1).

The aim of what follows is a preliminary working-out in four steps, from a strictly pragmatic point of view, of how the 'Sunday community' meeting at the week-end can reform itself in this way and work out a way of life based on the gospel that would cover the whole of life.[4] The basis for this practical theory of the Christian community is provided by a critique of the sociological and theological theories of leisure[2] and of the restriction of Church communities to the Sunday meeting for worship at the week-end.[3] This constructive criticism can only be grasped against the background provided by exposing the myth that holds the modern bourgeois world in subjection, the myth of man's realisation of himself through work as a social reality.

1. THE MYTH OF SOCIETY'S SELF-REALISATION AND ITS FACTUAL BASIS

Up until the 1970s the social sciences and trade union policies thought they could take as their starting-point the fact that in the industrialised countries the time devoted to work had dropped dramatically since the First World War by comparison with all earlier civilistions of mankind and that in the near future it could go on being shortened still further thanks to the introduction of new technologies.[2] From this point of view the restriction of the time devoted to work seemed to have won for people what qualitatively was a totally new dimension of life—leisure. Research into leisure, which began at the turn of the century and which has shown an explosive growth over the past two decades,[3] defined this new private dimension negatively on the one had as a time freed from the alienating limitations of work and on the other hand in a Utopian sense as providing room for fresh experiences, for self-realisation, for communication, for social integration, for fantasy, for play, for creative life, etc.

But the attractive appearance given by this complementary balancing of work and leisure turns out to be deceptive. Describing leisure as free time or spare time—the German term, *Freizeit*, means literally 'free time'—suggests that for the modern bourgeois there exists, besides the world of the essential production of goods, another world of freedom and leisure. Before examining this ideology of leisure with regard to the importance of its contents for the Christian community, it would be as well first to correct its factual basis.

(a) Working hours before and since the industrial revolution

Historical studies of the amount of time devoted to work by slaves in ancient Greece and Rome show, just as do studies of the amount of time devoted to work in the European middle ages,[4] that before the industrial revolution people did not work any longer than an employee working under agreed conditions of work in 1970 or thereabouts. The time devoted to work was restricted to a reasonable proportion by the existence of over 150 feast-days and by the natural limitation of darkness at night. It was only artificial light, machine production and the interests of capital in the early industrial phase that led to the exploitation and slavery of a working week of up to eighty hours, to the abolition of feast-days and the bitter struggle to replace them by time off and holidays for recreation. Moreover, the detailed analysis of how people spend their leisure shows that the major part of the time that has now been won from work has to be filled with activities that resemble work and are absolutely necessary: travelling to work, technical maintenance of cars, lawnmowers, and photographic dark-rooms, etc., shopping, moonlighting, further education, paperwork, etc. In fact men and women today have significantly less time for recreation, leisure and doing what they want to do than even the dependent workers of all pre-industrialised civilisations. Even from the quantitative point of view leisure emerges as the Utopia of the wage-slaves of industrial society, while it should be borne in mind that it is safe to hazard the guess that managers and executives today work hours as long as were worked in the last century only by the exploited proletariat.

(b) The meaning of work and enjoyment before and since the rise of the bourgeoisie

For the agricultural economy of the ancient world and the middle ages with its associated handicrafts, work meant first of all a burden, an exertion that was anything but desired, indeed even a 'curse' entailed by banishment from the imagined paradise (see Gen. 2-3). The Greek and Latin terms for work and business at the same time denoted the effort, distress and hardship (*ergon, labor*) or the negative aspect in contrast to leisure (*a-scholia, neg-otium*). The aim of all work and exertion lay beyond all this activity in repose, the fullness of peace (*shalom*), the relaxation of contemplation (*eidenai*) or the enjoyment of life (*fruitio*). In contrast to this the pioneer of political philosophy in the modern world, Thomas Hobbes, clearsightedly indicated in the seventeenth century what the bourgeois's enjoyment consisted of in the age of burgeoning colonialism, the expansion of trade, and the universal spread of a monetary economy. Not repose but movement was what satisfied the bourgeois striving after the acquisition of property: *vita motus est perpetuus*,[5] life is perpetual motion. For this kind of possessive-minded bourgeois pleasure is in fact his greed, and since 'appetite presupposes a farther end, there can be no contentment but in proceeding'.[6] Progress as such becomes the goal, which means that the goal of repose can no longer be found in the rhythm of life: 'Felicity, therefore (by which we mean continual delight), consisteth not in having prospered, but in prospering.'[7] Ambition for power impels towards becoming continually more powerful, towards the principle of competition and achievement, this sensual pleasure of the modern bourgeois bent on expansion: 'Continually to out-go the next before, is felicity.'[8] In an age determined by a purely monetary economy *homo faber* finds his happiness in exertion itself, he becomes the 'artificer of his own happiness', he must (to use the terms in which this fundamental tendency was expressed by the philosophy of German idealism) 'realise' or 'fulfil' himself.

Just as the bourgeois dependent on capital must, with his ability to work for others, sell his life for the endless expansion of the national economy, so he expends his mental and intellectual energies in the continual task of social self-realisation. He may no longer leave any existing relationships as they are: in order to realise and fulfil himself, he must even (following the work demanded of him by psychoanalysis) compass the psychological death of the first persons with whom he has established a relationship, his parents, in order to bring about a new relationship towards them; in the wake of the dissolution of the traditional family structure he must continually re-create afresh his 'love', which has been reduced to its purely private elements, without being able to come to rest in its firm embrace; and from this activity, moving restlessly from one relationship to the next, he can never cease. Just as the financial reward for his work and labour impels him towards continuous consumption, so can any self-realisation in the network of social communication and relationships no longer bring him peace: the sense of meaning of life seems to lie in continuous consumption. In keeping with the consistency with which in the nineteenth century Thomas Carlyle celebrated work as religion and religious life as work ('to work is to pray'), so too more recent theories of interaction in late capitalist society are equally consistent in interpreting our language, our psychological relationships (mother-child) and socialisation as the results of productive achievements, and thus in seeing the whole of life as the work of society.[9] This work brings about a continuous revolution in all relationships, all circumstances, and everything inherited from the past. The work wrought by society gives the bourgeois world that revolutionary character that Marx and Engels saw as fundamental to the capitalist mode of production of all social relationships: 'The bourgeoisie cannot exist without . . . bringing about a continuous revolution in all the relationships of society. . . . The incessant changes in production, the uninterrupted convulsion of the entire state of affairs of society, the perpetual insecurity and movement distinguish the epoch of the bourgeoisie from all others.'[10] In this revolutionary process it is only through his dealings, his activity and his productivity that the individual achieves his worth and dignity: he has become radically alienated from the God who is himself active, the Lord of history borne witness to in the Bible; he must bring about his own fulfilment himself without the help of grace.

2. SOCIOLOGICAL AND THEOLOGICAL THEORIES OF LEISURE

In considering a practical theory of celebration, worship and the life of the Christian community from a theological point of view, what is important is not only a realisation of the dominance that has been achieved by social relationships based on production and by the corresponding myth of self-realisation and self-fulfilment, but also the disenchantment with the various ideologies of leisure that is to be found in the highly industrialised countries of the West. The question is whether for a bourgeoisie busy with producing itself there can be anything at all beyond the world of work, as is implied by the concepts of leisure and free time. Does the leisure that people enjoy at the week-end and on holiday provide as it were the natural opportunity to become aware of and benefit from freedom, from redeemed existence, from peace, joy and redemption, so that this period of leisure would give the Christian community a jumping-off point for becoming aware of God's presence, reconciliation and peace? Can leisure be something like a *praeambula fidei*, a preparatory stage before actual belief, for proclaiming the gospel in industrial society?

In fact right at the start of the industrial age the philosopher of the bourgeois revolution, G. W. F. Hegel, celebrated religion as the 'Sunday of life' when nations escaped the harshness of the world of work and created a representation of freedom from the finite.[11] Although the young Marx quickly exposed this idealistic Sunday of the emotions as casting a halo over the unholy world of production, in his later work—even if without the slightest hint of religion—he too dreamed of a dimension beyond material production, of a genuine life that has leisure as its starting-point: 'The realm of freedom does in fact begin at the point where work, which is determined by necessity and the need to conform to external demands, ceases.' Even the rational form of work of the socialised man or woman 'remains . . . a realm of necessity. It is beyond this that there begins the development of human powers that sees itself as an end in itself, the true realm of freedom. . . '.[12] In a way that is structurally similar Leo XIII in *Rerum novarum* regards work as a burden and an affliction to be borne by mankind, with the result that the way to true life can only begin beyond the time devoted to work during the freedom from work on Sunday. This Sunday rest 'should be rest from labour, hallowed by religion. Rest (combined with religious observances) disposes man to forget for a while the business of his everyday life, to turn his thoughts to things heavenly, and to the worship which he so strictly owes to the Eternal Godhead.' By lying beyond the time devoted to work Sunday thus symbolised that next world in which true life was to begin after our exile here on earth.[13]

In all these contrasts between leisure and the time devoted to work, work remains the negative element which can only be overcome beyond it. But this simple opposition between leisure and work—characteristic of all conservative theories of leisure—exhibits two fundamental defects. First of all it overlooks the fact that in all industrial States the use of leisure remains from the socio-economic point of view determined by the cycle of production and thus by the process of work. Thus writing within the context of the Soviet bloc G. Grušin describes as the central concern of policies for leisure 'the education and self-education of the human personality'. Hence society must 'continually *work* to educate and re-educate the personality, to *develop further* its cultural potential (mental and physical, intellectual and emotional, ideological and ethical), to *change* the human personality's taste and demands. It is only in this way that the problem of the use of leisure can be solved.'[14] The same prescription is to be found in a western context when H. Schelsky urges the 'formation of the person and of the human being' along with 'systematic distraction' [*sic*] as a way of using leisure to 'complement the one-sided development and burdening of mankind that occurs in work'.[15] These conservative architects of leisure overlook the fact that the self-fulfilment they advocate through the use of consumption and leisure remains completely within the context of social production and thus within the sphere of work. As Habermas has rightly pointed out,[16] the function of this kind of leisure remains bound to its opposite, work: its purpose is simply to allow one's capacity to work to recuperate, to compensate for the physical exhaustion and nervous wear-and-tear caused by work, and to afford a temporary escape from the dependence and frustrations experienced in work. Corresponding to this first defect of such theories of leisure is the second: they are unable to indicate any conditions under which the social process of work can itself be transformed into a communicative, social and liberating activity. They are content to leave things as they are in order to find fulfilment beyond them. But this is in fact the great illusion of ideologies of leisure: for as long as the man or woman actively involved in work can himself or herself find in his or her own activity no fulfilment, no freedom and no sense, so long is he or she equally unable to find such fulfilment beyond or outside work in his or her leisure time that is by definition free from work. Whether the life of the Christian community, with its emphasis on Sunday worship, can provide room for the liberating and redeeming alternative to time spent in work offered by the message of the Old and New Testaments is a question that must now be gone into in greater detail.

3. 'THE DAY OF THE LORD'

(a) The meaning of the Jewish Sabbath

Every arrangement of time on a strongly rhythmical pattern with regularly recurring feast-days corresponds to a particular rationalisation of working life. Food-gathering and hunting cultures before the emergence of the State, as well as most nomadic peoples, are ignorant of the working week with its regular pauses: times for doing nothing and the long festival periods were fixed by priests or tribal chieftains according to the changing constellations of the sky. Characteristic for these festivals are the return of the ancestors, fertility rites, the consumption of goods and ritual battle, while magic rituals enable all forms of work outside these periods to be controlled in a highly 'rational' manner.[17]

In contrast to this cosmic rhythm underlying the events of life, the pattern of the Jewish Sabbath, which emerged at the latest after the Exile, appears as the first attempt in the ancient world to impose a rigid pattern of time: the seven-day week makes the periods of work and worship independent of the phases of sun, moon and stars. This strongly rationalised pattern of periods of work and rest no longer symbolises the rhythm of nature but sets the rhythm of worship marked by the Sabbath in opposition to it. To the extent that this rigid rhythm of seven expresses the order of creation in the priestly theology (Exod. 20:11, 31:17), it is contrasting the pattern of worship with chaos and setting it above every cosmic order; to the extent that, following the theology of Deuteronomy (Deut. 5:15), the seventh day becomes a memorial of the Exodus and of being set free from Egypt, it sets up against the compulsion of work God's action of liberation from the entire situation of work; and to the extent finally that it is prophetically evoked as a symbol of the covenant (Ezek. 20:12, 20) this day of the Lord symbolises Israel's basic structure as the people of Yahweh.

With a period of rest coming to express God's action in the realm of history, a more exact definition now emerges of what precisely is meant by 'work'. Thus the Book of Jubilees establishes the following activities as 'works' forbidden on the Sabbath under pain of death: business transactions and journeys, drawing water and transporting goods, preparing foodstuffs, travelling and tilling a plot of land, kindling fire and loading beasts of burden, travelling by sea, fighting and waging war, slaughtering and capturing animals.[18] To the extent that the time free from such activities became an expression of God's creative, liberating and redeeming activity, there grew precisely the danger that is to be found in contemporary ideologies of leisure, namely that the period of normal everyday life and work was no longer able to represent the real nature, the sense and the liberating basis of the entire process of life. Inasmuch as certain activities were forbidden on the day of the Lord, they became desacralised, made profane, they became mere work. The prophetic criticism of the concentration on worship in itself presupposes this division and attempts once more to draw the social activities of everyday life into a fundamental relationship with Yahweh's loyal, gracious and merciful activity.

(b) Jesus' criticism of the Jewish Sabbath

Jesus' criticism of the Sabbath concerns the core of his message and his doings; indeed, according to Mark 3:6 and the parallel passages, it led to his opponents' decision to compass his death. But it can become clear where the significance of this radical criticism lies only if the entire Sabbath saying of Mark 2:27-28 is read in the way that it is proclaimed by the New Testament as the gospel of Jesus Christ (and thus without dividing verse 27 from verse 28 as historical criticism would have us do): 'The sabbath was made for man, not man for the sabbath; so the Son of Man is lord even of the sabbath.' As is shown by Jesus' healing on the Sabbath (Mark 3:1-6 and parallels; Luke 13:10-17, 14:1-6; John 5:1-18, 9:1-41) in connection with his proclamation (Luke 4:21), Jesus Christ's actions bring about the 'day of the lord' promised by the prophets (Isa. 61:2), and this means the Messianic fulfilment.[19] The Son of Man who fulfils Yahweh's action in history is Lord over all time, and therefore he frees those who are his own for the original pattern of things in which all time belongs to mankind because all time means a time of salvation, a perpetual 'today' of the salvation that is breaking in upon us in Jesus Christ (see Heb. 3-4).

Jesus Christ's fullness of power over the end of time is shown by the fact that before God he demolishes the barriers of time devoted to work and time devoted to rest and that, as is shown by the parables, he opens up the world of everyday life as the time for God's loyal, merciful and just presence. Jesus' action of reconciliation (see Luke

5:17-26) tolerates no restriction to particular days and festive seasons: 'My father is working still, and I am working' (John 5:17). Through the Lord of history, the crucified one who has been raised up, the day of the Lord has become the criterion of all historical time: the time ruled by this Lord is at all times set free for freedom, which means that it is also set free for a form of work set free from the curse of having to bring about one's own fulfilment.

In his letter to the Galatians (4:8-11) Paul sharply attacks all who observe days, months, seasons and years, and thus the Jewish liturgical calendar: they serve the elemental spirits of the universe and not the Lord. Redemption from the curse of the law means redemption in Jesus Christ for the new creation (2 Cor. 5:17; Gal. 6:15); but in this there is no longer any obligation to the Sabbath (Col. 2:16-17), but only a continual living in Jesus Christ for God. This life is not something that has to be worked out and realised but rather rests entirely in what God himself has wrought in us in Jesus Christ. For Paul it is self-evident that this liberating Word of God itself leads once again to action and makes possible work in the service of the community: what he is preaching is not enthusiasm for a religious élite but salvation from the powers of the secular age, something which itself makes possible action freed from these powers of the law, of sin and of death. What is decisive for the Christian pattern of time is thus not to be found in the fact that Christians may now work on the Sabbath as well as on other days, but in the fact that all working is understood as charism, as activity in Jesus Christ that expresses solidarity and liberation. 'The new law,' someone as early as Justin was to lay down, 'demands that you celebrate the Sabbath continually.'[20] The meaning expressed by the Jewish Sabbath—the order of creation, liberation from the slavery of forced labour, and the covenant with Israel's Lord—is thus transcended in the triple Hegelian sense: abolished in its restriction to free time, maintained in its meaning and extended to cover the whole of time.

(c) The vicissitudes of the Christian Lord's Day

As is well known, the Christians made a working day, the day *after* the Sabbath, the day of the Lord, and up until the recodification of their faith in legal forms that set in from the fourth century on they did not celebrate a 'Sunday' but rather established their community on a weekday by celebrating the Eucharist.[21] The realm of the lordship of Christ that was awaited at the end of time was for them congruent with the realm of the everyday world. But by incorporating its liturgical calendar into the pattern inherited from the administration of the Roman Empire from Constantine on, the Church took over at the same time the letter's rhythm of work based on the planetary week and cosmically oriented, and thus took over the day of the sun as the day of the Lord. This fundamental restriction of Christian time to one day brought in its wake, between the fourth and the eighth centuries, a new and rigid application to the Christian Sunday of the Old Testament prescriptions with regard to the Sabbath, in the course of which from the time of Charlemagne at the latest the ban on servile work on Sunday which is still in force became decisive. However strongly Martin Luther in particular argued on theological grounds against this Sabbatarianism and thus sought to allow the time devoted to work to be once more penetrated by Christianity, through abolishing the legal prescriptions pertaining to Sunday, nevertheless even the Reformation was able to do little to hold back this rationalised division between working time and the Church's festive seasons. This division fitted in far too well with the modern rage for work and the corresponding need for a regular period of recuperation, as did the accompanying restriction of the religious way of life to Sunday, for any attempt to disrupt it to be able to succeed, as is shown in particular by all the failed attempts (France, 1906; USSR, 1940) to introduce other rhythms of work.

In view of the still intact myth of the world of work in those societies of high technology which, at the expense of the underdevelopment of the majority of the earth's regions and at the expense of their own capacity for life, have turned all relationships into relationships of production and consumption, the question arises how the Christian community can present its gospel of the Lord's time of grace, of liberation for freedom in Jesus Christ and can obtain a hearing for this universal time of work.

4. THE WORKADAY AND THE SUNDAY COMMUNITY

(a) The community of the Lord and communication among members

Every Christian community is continually established anew through the Word, Jesus Christ, who dispenses himself in the words of proclamation and in the bread of life: this word establishes communion, the community of the Lord. This fundamental procedure of the acceptance of God's articulate action, which in the worship of the community establishes a visible unity out of people who form anything but a unity (employees and employers, conservatives and socialists, old and young, the unemployed and those with too much to do, women and men, natives and foreigners), does not lead to unification in Christ if the point of reference that links all these various individuals together remains the *liturgus*, the pastor. The *communio* of the Lord who gives himself calls for the communication in solidarity of those who are summoned by him to form a community. Nor do prayer in common and singing together, with the unity that that can create, suffice. Rather the community must enter into verbal communication among its members, and do so within its service of worship by means of an increase in the use of lay preachers, including women and outsiders, by means of lay people contributing to the intercessions, the preparation of the service, and leading the congregation in prayer, and by means of lay people sharing in the distribution of communion and *all* young people (not just those who are boys) acting as altar servers; in addition the surroundings in which services are held must make it possible for people to greet and meet each other after the service. The Lord's giving of himself in his Word with his body demands more than a private response in the individualised devotion of the Sunday congregation: the response it is looking for is a community marked by solidarity and communication.

(b) The covering of the whole social reality by the Christian community

But even the transformation of the nuclear parish into a community marked by communication remains alien to the gospel if it does not intervene in the processes of work and social relationships by means of symbolic actions. Of course the Christian community cannot in an as it were theocratic manner bring about a complete and universal change in the structures of society and in productive relationships; but as long as it does not as a community show its solidarity by working for those who are left on one side in these processes of production and socialisation, those who are pushed to one side as representing a weakening of productive effort, those who despair of self-fulfilment or those who are excluded from productive society (the old, the mentally and physically ill, the handicapped, prisoners, refugees, alcoholics, drug addicts, overburdened mothers, problem children, foreigners), as long as it is not at least working away at the creation of a single social reality, it remains the community of those who claim the Lord for themselves, a community of salvation-capitalists and the self-justified. The reality of the Eucharist cannot lead to an encounter with the Lord if this Lord is not found where he himself let himself be placed by his cross: in the prisons, in the situation of the stranger, the naked, the hungry, the thirsty (Matt. 25:31-46). It is only through its symbolic actions of solidarity that the nuclear parish can make contact with those believers who are to be found on its margins and outside it. What would be desirable would be for every parish to undertake without interruption at least one kind of social work within its own locality and one symbolic campaign beyond it (such as linking up with a parish in the Third World, work for Amnesty International or for the international peace work of Pax Christi, etc.). It is only in this way that it will come to a social awareness of the connections between the message of the kingdom of God and the world of production as it exists in reality with all its forms of repression and its opportunities.

(c) The parish as mission—force rather than recipient of salvation

Within the context of the social administration and functional organisation that mark the forms of society in industrial countries, the parish itself threatens to become merely the place where salvation is administered. In addition, the rational power-structure of the Catholic hierarchy tends towards bureaucratic organisation. However efficient this may be when it comes to the liturgy and administration, it equally threatens to absorb into itself the internal consequences and implications of God's communication of himself in Jesus Christ's giving of himself in the Eucharist and in the Word, and thus to squeeze out the missionary consequences and implications of the message of God's gracious action in history. In practice Catholics have long since dispensed themselves from the missionary task laid upon them by baptism and confirmation; and they have done so because the parish structure reduced them to passive recipients of regularly administered doses of salvation, because their proper task of proclaiming the gospel in the family and at work and beyond was no longer confided and entrusted to them. It is only in the new churches and in the many small Protestant churches that lay people find that their missionary vocation is accepted. But the mission of the parish should once again become something other than the old-style parish mission—which again made the laity merely the recipients of the mission conducted by the clergy. The plain meaning of the gospel is that the good of faith that has been entrusted to us can only stay alive if it is handed on, if it is proclaimed to non-believers and lived out for their benefit. The Sunday community's inner life will determine its everyday life to the extent that its leader together with its members hands the gospel on through missionary activity. This may sound Utopian when applied to the established churches of industrialised countries; but that is an indictment against them and the bureaucratic rigidity in which they have become set and which excludes all eschatological tension. What is needed here is not just to pay lip-service to the new theology of the participation of the laity in Christ's threefold office as expressed by Vatican II and John Paul II but to take it seriously with a view to the structural reform that the Catholic Church needs.[22]

(d) Holidays as laboratories of freedom

The practice of regular holidays that is characteristic of our way of life[23] may not, because of its nature of consumption and its functions as a means of improving efficiency, represent a dimension of freedom, it may not transform the individual, rooted in his desire for self-fulfilment and in productivity, into a liberated human being, but at the same time it offers a realm within which Christian communities can suggest and try out alternative ways of life. What formerly were highly intellectual exercises often reserved for an élite can today become Christian holiday communities living an alternative way of life (Taizé, for example, offers such an alternative for many people). Here alternatives to work seen as efficient achievement, to alienation from the natural world and to the division of labour can be developed in connection with the gospel message of the new creation, not in highly organised 'cities of God' and not as planned Utopias, but in association with alternative forms of life drawing on anthropological, socialist and monastic sources as a realm for social learning by Christians who in their well-run churches have never experienced community, renunciation of consumption, playful interaction, work in common, and the charismatic exposition of the gospel.

(e) The interaction of worship and social life through everyday events

Every proposal for parish renewal itself stands under the danger of new demands for efficient achievement and under the pressure of a Christianity that is as it were the product of active creation. What must be emphasised in contrast to this is that the interaction of worship and social life comes into play precisely when the community is stimulated into social learning and work by the simplest of everyday events—a strike in the neighbourhood, employees being made redundant, a dispute over new educational proposals, the isolation of older citizens, the calling up of Christians for military service, the exclusion of handicapped children from ordinary schools, etc. Young people do not need some Catholic Sunday event planned on an enormous scale but somewhere for their discos, a service of worship using the music and media they are used to, and a community leader who is concerned primarily to serve their interests and not his own self-importance. The parish has an important function primarily in the transmission of social communication and its integration into the action of the liturgy. It cannot itself organise Christian life in the differentiated settings of family, school, workplace, sport, politics, etc., but it can open up social links by symbolically working away at individual everyday events in the spirit of the gospel.

(f) The importance of education and its integration with living

As research into leisure has shown, consumption of the mass media, the choice of activities during leisure and on holiday, and ability for social action depend essentially on the level of general education. Education makes connections visible, broadens the ability to decide, and makes people better able to communicate. As long as theological education, in keeping with the division of labour, represents nothing but a cerebral and intellectual acquisition of knowledge of the Christian tradition and fails to integrate Christian action in the contexts of modern social relationships and the world of work, the economic development and the political realities of the world as a whole, the teachers of religion and community leaders of the future cannot get this necessary education under way. Social education in any case demands more than the cumulative learning of harmonised facts: it demands at least a gesture towards working out the content of education against the reality of society itself. Hence what is needed is for theology students to be brought into the social work of Christian parishes and their sociological and theological reflection, in the service of communities that aim at doing more than transmitting the liturgy on one hand and school-learning on the other.

The decisive question for Christian parishes squeezed into the leisure time left over from work remains whether in their proclamation, social service, education and social interaction they become capable of breaking the myth of production and self-fulfilment in order symbolically to make room for God's action in Jesus Christ.

Translated by Robert Nowell

Notes

1. Karl Marx, Friedrich Engels *Werke* XXV (Berlin 1977) p. 838.
2. Thus for example O. von Nell-Breuning and K. Erlinghagen *s.v. Freizeit* in *Handwörterbuch der Sozialwissenschaften* (Stuttgart 1965) IV pp. 138-143.
3. As an introduction, see B. M. Berger *The Sociology of Leisure: Industrial Relations I* (1962); S. de Grazia *Of Time, Work and Leisure* (New York 1962); E. O. Smigel, ed. *Work and Leisure* (New Haven 1963); A. Szalai *The Use of Time* (Paris 1972); M. Kaplan *Leisure* (New York 1975); J. Dumazedier *Vers une civilisation du loisir?* (Paris 1962); J. Fourastié *Des loisirs: pour qui faire?* (Tournai 1970); C. A. Andrae *Ökonomik der Freizeit* (Reinbek 1970); G. Bally *Vom Spielraum der Freiheit* (Basle 1966); G. Eichler *Spiel und Arbeit* (Stuttgart 1979); G. Grušin *Die freie Zeit als Problem* (East Berlin 1970); J. Habermas 'Soziologische Notizen zum Verhältnis von Arbeit und Freizeit' in *Konkrete Vernunft: Festschrift für E. Rothacker* (Bonn 1958) 219-231; H. Kluth *Freizeit im Schatten der industriellen Arbeit* (Göttingen 1966); E. Küng *Arbeit und Freizeit in der nachindustriellen Gesellschaft* (Tübingen 1971); W. Nahrstedt *Die Entstehung der Freizeit* (Göttingen 1972); H. W. Opaschowski *Pädagogik der Freizeit* (Bad Heilbrunn 1973); E. K. Scheuch, ed. *Soziologie der Freizeit* (Gütersloh 1972); A. Timm *Verlust der Musse* (Hamburg 1968).
4. See E. Weber *Das Freizeitproblem* (Munich/Basle 1963); H. L. Wilensky 'The uneven distribution of leisure' in E. O. Smigel, ed. *Work and Leisure* (New Haven 1963) 107-145; S. de Grazia *Of Time, Work and Leisure* (New York 1962).
5. Thomas Hobbes *Opera Philosophica* edited G. Molesworth (London 1839-1845, reprinted Aalen 1966) II p. 103.
6. Thomas Hobbes *The Elements of Law, natural and politic,* edited F. Tönnies, 2nd ed. M. M. Goldsmith (London 1969) p. 30.
7. *Ibid.* p. 30.
8. *Ibid.* p. 48.
9. See especially A. Lorenzer *Zur Begründung einer materialistischen Sozialisationstheorie* (Frankfurt-am-Main 1973).
10. See especially *Werke* IV pp. 462-468.
11. See G. W. F. Hegel *Vorlesungen über die Philosophie der Religion* I (Theorie-Werkausgabe XVI Frankfurt-am-Main 1969) pp. 12 ff.
12. Karl Marx, Friedrich Engels *Werke* XXV (Berlin 1977) p. 828.
13. Leo XIII *Rerum novarum* § 32, cf. §§ 14, 18, 42.
14. G. Grušin *Die freie Zeit als Problem* (East Berlin 1970) p. 76 (my italics).
15. H. Schelsky *Auf der Suche nach Wirklichkeit* (Düsseldorf/Cologne 1965) pp. 417-418.
16. See J. Habermas 'Soziologische Notizen zum Verhältnis von Arbeit und Freizeit' in *Konkrete Vernunft: Festschrift für E. Rothacker* (Bonn 1958) 224.
17. See B. Malinowski *Magic, Science and Religion* (New York 1948).
18. See The Book of Jubilees 2:29-30, 50:8-13; R. H. Charles *The Apocrypha and Pseudepigrapha of the Old Testament in English* (Oxford 1913) II pp. 15, 81-82.
19. On this and on what follows see W. Rordorf *Der Sonntag* (Zürich 1962) pp. 55-151.
20. *Dialogue with Trypho* 12:3.
21. On what follows see P. Eicher 'Der Tag des Herrn für die Sklaven der Arbeitszeit' in *Diakonia* 10 (1979) 3-11; W. Rordorf *Der Sonntag* (Zürich 1962); P. Cotten *From Sabbath to Sunday* (Bethlehem 1933); H. Dumaine art. 'Dimanche' in *Dictionnaire d'archéologie chrétienne* (Paris 1921) IV cols. 858-994; E. Schürer 'Die siebentägige Woche im Gebrauche der christlichen Kirche der ersten Jahrhunderte in *ZNW* 6 (1905) 1-66; F. J. Dölger 'Die Planetenwoche der griechisch-römischen Antike und der christliche Sonntag' in *Antike und Christentum* 6 (1941) 202-238.

22. See P. Eicher *Priester und Laien—im Wesen verschieden?* in G. Denzler, ed. *Priester für heute* (Munich 1980) 34-50.

23. For the practical loosening up of Sunday and holiday, see also P. Eicher *Der Herr gibt's den Seinen im Schlaf* (Munich 1980) pp. 91-106.

André Aubry

The Feast of Peoples and the Explosion of Society—Popular Practice and Liturgical Practice

IF IT IS true that liturgy is above all a celebration of the history of man's salvation, we are first and foremost confronted, in any consideration of the times of that celebration, with history itself and with such questions as: Within what history is liturgy celebrated? At what moment in history do various peoples celebrate their liturgy? To what 'times' do they aspire?

In the tropics, the time is not always Greenwich Mean Time and it is not always the same hour in the North as it is in the South. If it were, dialogue between the two hemispheres would not be so high on the agenda or so difficult and full of problems. It is obvious that the plans and hopes and even the eschatological expectations of different nations are in a state of tension.

As a result of this tension, I have deliberately chosen to examine liturgical practice and the successes and failures of liturgists in this article exclusively from the point of view of history.

1. THE 'TIME' OF THE THIRD WORLD

Given this restriction, it is important to state straightaway the environment within which I am working and which I shall therefore consider and discuss principally here. I am working among the Indian population of Chiapas on the Mexican side of the frontier with Guatemala. I do not say this because I want to entice the reader by exotic attractions, but simply in order to point out at the beginning of this article, for example, that the feast of the people of Nicaragua has been quite different from the feast for the western allies of Somoza. Yet it is precisely that feast which the Church in question and, in communion with it, many other churches celebrated. The hungry have been filled with good things only because the rich have left empty-handed and the mighty have come down from their thrones. The time of the people concerned was in conflict with the other time. The *in illo tempore* cannot be the time of Caesar. At the level of history, it is clear that the feast produces conflict and its celebration takes place in the comfort of 'cries of rejoicing and songs of victory', as in the psalms of Hallel.

Chiapas sits astride the historical seventeenth parallel which runs from Mexico through Ethiopia to Vietnam and has shaken recent western history from Zapata to Ho Chi Minh. The seventeenth parallel had given the Third World a new history either as a lived experience or sought in struggle. This issue of *Concilium* is devoted to an examination of the ways in which social change and liturgical celebration are linked. We have therefore, to begin with, to define as precisely as possible the social plan of these peoples.

As one who is situated in the Third World, not only in the South, but also at the lowest level of that world (in the basement of the social structure and in a state of peaceful solidarity with the 'damned of the earth'), I recognise that the desire for change cannot be confused with the attraction of 'development' in the capitalist and industrialist sense of the word that the First World is trying to make a universal aspiration. The plan of a 'contemporary world' to which my companions and allies aspire is not in accordance with the universe built of iron and steel and for the easy mental and physical circumstances of its inhabitants which the dominant nations have in mind. On the contrary, it is the 'plan of liberation' that Medellín identified as long ago as 1968 by comparing the traditional biblical history of salvation with the historical struggle of movements working for liberation. The social plan pointing to the emergence of a completely new man, envisaged by the peoples of the Third World and glimpsed by Paul, Che Guevara, Franz Fanon and so many others engaged in struggle is confused, in the density of three continents and the demographic turmoil of two-thirds of the world's population, with a universal uprising of peasants resisting and protesting and fighting against the imperialist, western model of urban industrialised development.

The time of the First World was, of course, the nineteenth century, when towns were arising, strong and triumphant, everywhere and the countryside was stripped. Northern industry used up the sources of energy and the raw materials of the Third World. The identity of that world was hidden from view by colonialism.

Since the beginning of the twentieth century, however, that identity has made itself felt increasingly powerfully on history. This movement began in Mexico and China. It extended to Cuba and Algeria, the Middle East and Vietnam and later reached, to name only a few examples, Angola and Nicaragua. In all these different places, peasants took part in the struggle and have been victorious, regarding their rights from the domination and 'modern' urban way of life in the West. The out of date opposition between town and country has been overcome for ever, in an attempt to create a society that is quite new and non-aligned—a society with which the future of the peoples of the Third World can be truly identified.[1]

With all this in mind, we have a clear picture of what the feast is at the social level of a people in the modern world, bearing in mind the relationships that exist between the feast of peoples and social change. Above all, that feast expresses what is anticipated in that people's struggles and provides a prophetic image of the man who is being born among that people. It is, moreover, already celebrating that new man in the creative Utopia or as an eschatological desire. At a different level, the historical reality is also apparent—the present struggle and the social situation in which that people is placed and is struggling here and now.

But this is precisely where the deep uneasiness of our liturgy is most acutely felt. Despite the Second Vatican Council, that liturgy is still a Roman liturgy, in other words, a liturgy of the First World. It follows the patterns of a different 'time' and a different history. It is an alien liturgy, in agreement with the world of the oppressors and in conflict with that of the oppressed.

2. THE LITURGY AS A POLITICAL PROBLEM

The Third World peoples are inclined as a whole to suspect that this liturgy, which is clearly imported, is a form of cultural invasion or neo-colonial penetration. Its God has all the attributes of a lord and master who needs 'servants' (serfs) and the 'world' only enters, despite all the attempts made in the language of the liturgy, as a potential 'presence' of the Church, at least when it is not overcome by the Church. The 'peace' of the Eucharistic prayers or the prayers is semantically shaped by the *pax romana*, which means that it points to the peace brought by the imperialists of the West. Finally, the 'poor' of the liturgy are an object of compassion and not the oppressed who are to create a new society.

This gives rise to a paradox. This liturgical way of speaking is no longer always a true expression of the practice of men in the First World who are often socially uneasy and have spoken out on behalf of Vietnam in the United States or on the side of the Algerians in France and have even been sent to prison because of what they have said and done. This same liturgical language does, however, continue to sustain other First World men who were not born in the West, but who still form part of the ruling classes in the Third World, where they claim to represent the dynamic 'modernised' or 'developed' society of which they are still dreaming. This impotent liturgy reflects—and probably reproduces—a similarly old and impotent society and leaves those who follow it without an identity. They either submit or cling to it.

Even officially, the Church has recognised the existence of this uneasiness. That is why adaptation (the Roman vocabulary), or an incarnation in native cultures (the Latin-American vocabulary), is permitted under the new arrangements. These possibilities are dubious reflections of an attitude towards native cultures in which the orthodox anthropological approach of the American type has become bogged down. These initiatives, however, have come about as a result of gaps in 'missionary' endeavour. For this reason, there is an ethnocentric choice of cultural terms and the western attempts to recover what has been lost are regularly rejected by the Third World peoples, who now do not want their cultural identity to be watered down or falsified.

I shall not consider the problem of the feast as a liturgical matter, but rather as the basis for social reflection. The feast is, after all, the product of a society and its rightful expression. As its own product, it gives it an identity as a society (it is its 'trade mark'; it is 'made in . . .') and, as its expression of itself, it can only be deciphered by the decoding mechanisms of its own language. Every society is open to change, but its language is not created by effort—on the contrary, it is received and assimilated and no hierarchy or generous proposal can enforce acceptance of a liturgical language or change it. A renewed liturgy can only arise from a group of new men to whom the society that they are recreating has given birth—an event that takes place in the action itself which transforms that society. At the same time, that act of transformation also bequeaths a language which fashions the men themselves and no one is in control of it (because, if it were to change at the will of those who spoke it, it would become mere gibberish and be understood by no one at all).

In this socio-cultural interchange, the feast is kept as a pure expression of the society in question by its language. If the language of celebration (not only the verbal, but also the symbolic language) continues, for example, to be that of the dominant classes, then an oligarchical form of society is postulated by the feast. If, on the other hand, it is that of the dominated and oppressed classes, it will result in a feast prophesying a social struggle which will 'put down the mighty from their thrones'.

From whatever point of view it is seen, the feast is never innocent or—and this comes to the same thing—it is only as innocent as the society that it expresses, causes to continue or builds. Although it tries to protect itself from it, the liturgy always has a political flavour derived from its language, strong or weak according to the degree with which it is identified with the dominant or dominated classes. This idea will be thrown into much sharper light when we try to glimpse the content of the feast of the peasant peoples through its language. For the present, however, we have simply to note that there are many historical examples pointing to abundant phenomenological evidence.

On the one hand, the 'official' or 'military' masses celebrated by and for the oligarchy and privileged classes have long been a familiar practice in the history of the Church. The scars of this liturgy are still to be seen on churches in the Third World. On the façade of the church of Santo Domingo de San Cristóbal de Las Casas, for example, a masterpiece of colonial baroque architecture, there is the eagle with two heads of the Bourbon empire. Even worse, on the façade of the church of the same name at Oaxaca, also in Mexico, there are figures of a conquistador in military uniform and a Dominican friar, both representing the Church in the political symbolism of the time: 'the sword and the holy water sprinkler'.

On the other hand, there have in recent years been many clandestine Masses celebrated by and for the oppressed classes in Nazi concentration camps and in prisons. There was also, for example, the subversive, ecumenical Eucharist of Pentecost celebrated in Paris in May 1968. Also in 1968, the first concelebrated Mass was celebrated at Bilbao by young Basque priests who were members of ETA—a feast of which a record was made—and, again in 1968, a very moving Eucharist was celebrated during the course of an immense gathering of people in Puerto Rico. After the homily, Bishop Parrilla celebrated the hundredth anniversary of the Cry of Independence of Lares by solemnly burning his American passport and lighting the candles on the altar with this improvised torch. Then there was the Mass during which Mario Gamo, the priest, was arrested in Madrid by Franco's police in 1969. There was also the astonishing strike of the Mass of the whole diocese of Riobamba (in Ecuador) in 1971, after the arrest or the expulsion of two of the diocesan priests, creating a real political problem for the governor of the province.[2]

Since then, there have been other important centres where this liturgy has been celebrated. On many occasions it had been celebrated by Mgr Oscar Romero in the Cathedral of San Salvador. At his funeral, the armed forces of the Junta shot hundreds of people at the time of the liturgical celebration. After having concelebrated the Eucharist on the occasion of the town's four hundred and fiftieth anniversary at the Cathedral of San Cristóbal de Las Casas in Mexico with the Apostolic Delegate and several other bishops, Mgr Samuel Ruíz was confronted, as he was leaving the building, by a planter with a revolver in his hand. This happened in March 1978. Finally, a great Eucharist of liberation was celebrated at the recently renamed city of Ciudad Sandino in Nicaragua, in what was previously known as Open 3 (Managua). This has become a regular weekly liturgical practice at Cuernavaca in Mexico and the press always reports the liberation Masses celebrated by the Bishop of Cuernavaca, Don Sergio Méndez Arceo.

3. THE FEAST OF THE PEASANTS

Let us, however, now return to the question of the peasants living on the seventeenth parallel. These people are not always politically conscious, but their feast does contain a certain political charge which is able at times to explode into revolution (as in Iran).

It is fundamentally a great, popular, country feast. The village leaders, both civil and religious, are put in prison if they do not attend and the people themselves—men, women and children—are there in great numbers, representing their own neighbour-hood and thus drawing attention to the civic importance of the 'democratic' organisation. Strangers, outsiders, traders and visitors also come, since 'it would not be a real feast if everyone were not invited'. These outsiders are punished if they do not behave properly. If, on the other hand, they do not provoke incidents, they are treated warmly and with great hospitality. A watch is kept on the proceedings by a group of 'policemen'. They are armed with batons, but they behave discreetly. Missing the feast is a denial of one's citizenship, while visiting the village at the time of the feast is regarded as a friendly gesture of solidarity.

The signs of this feast are the elegance of the clothes for the 'ceremonies' (social rituals), 'spirits' for the social relationships, meetings (for example, at a 'leader's' house), meals (frequently symbolic and even ritual in character, always sober yet served with alcohol) and, of course, the great gatherings of people. The latter include buying and selling at the market, family and diplomatic reconciliations, opinion sounding concerning plans of general interest and long visits to the church, which is richly decorated outside and in for the feast. The whole feast is accompanied constantly by music, sung and played at various points. The musicians have a social function and if they try to avoid it they are subjected to certain penalties.

The feast itself is offered by the authorities who are responsible for it—the major-domo of the patron saint is, for example, one of those authorities. Within the space of a few days, he may spend all his capital on popular merry-making and at the end of the festivities be completely ruined, that is to say, he is reduced to the ranks of poverty once again. Although, in practice, the casuistic law of 'caciquism' comes into operation with the result that a restoration of equality among the people is resisted, the ideal is that equality should in fact be restored.

This social plan is acknowledged by a reversal of normal situations. The day-labourer in the plantations, if he is given a responsibility at the feast, is respected by his fellow-villagers with the deference that is in accordance with his great dignity. The person who normally enjoys the highest authority, on the other hand, can be criticised and even mocked during the feast, provided that this is done with good humour and in a quasi-ritual way in song and dance.

This classical inversion of the social order—which is also reflected in the practice of shooting at the great ones of this world as 'Aunt Sallies' in shooting booths on urban fair-grounds and the mockery of the police that forms an important part of the Punch and Judy Show, thus providing a safety valve for the maintenance of public order and society in general—touches on subversion on the part of the peasants. Colonialism imposed six prohibitions on the native peasant classes. (The dominant land-owning classes sometimes still insist on these prohibitions.) They were (and sometimes still are) a prohibition against the wearing of hats, which is the privilege of the colonialists and their successors; singing and dancing, which were regarded as pagan and were forbidden for centuries by the missionaries; the eating of meat, of which, it was claimed, 'the Indians must not be allowed to taste the flavour'; riding on horses, which would be an insult to the conquistador and his descendants; and the use of all forms of powder. The Spaniards forbade the natives most strictly to use the latter.

During the feast, however, many of these prohibitions are defied. Everyone wears a hat. These are decorated with ribbons when worn by someone in authority. The people's leaders sing and dance even in the sanctuary of the Church. Before the feast begins, a bull is specially chosen to be eaten at the meals. There are always tournaments and horse-racing on the public square. At night there are firework displays and crackers are let off, marking every stage of the feast.

The priest is only invited. He would not be invited again if he did not respect the procedure established by the villagers in authority. During Mass, he may often be irritated by various 'profanations' of the Eucharist, but he can only witness these without being able to prevent them. At the elevation of the Host, for example, the people may begin to incant or to dance. Other 'profanities' may include a 'concelebration' by little groups of people in authority at the feast, sitting on the ground with their commanders' sticks between their legs and a jug of spirits (for the drink-offering), a packet of cigarettes (for communion) and a perfume burner (for the ceremony).

The feast has often been the melting pot in which armed rebellion has been prepared. In the case of Chiapas, the district with which we are dealing here, rebellion broke out during the Feast of Our Lady of Charity in 1712, the Feast of the Saints of the Cave in 1869 and that of the Sacred Heart in 1911. These events are still told to the children today, on the eve of the feast.

4. THE PEASANTS' FEAST AS A SOCIAL 'TEXT' OR CONTEXT

All these syndromes and reactions are both civil and religious. The whole of peasant society is crystallised in them. It is only by a process of abstraction that the 'liturgical' aspect of these phenomena can be distinguished.

The liturgical action is always surrounded by a symbolic context which gives order and cohesion to the objects involved (a crucifix, perhaps, the statue of the saint, lighted candles, the alms to be distributed and so on), the places visited (an enclosure, a church or a cave), the times (the feast of the patron saint, carnival time and so on), the rites (incense, alcohol, processions, flowers, music, etc.) and the people taking part (the priest, the major-domo, the healer, the sick person, the one asking on his behalf, the adversary and others).

The city-dweller cannot understand the peasants' feast and thinks that it is primitive. The missionary denounces the syncretism present in its confusion of aspects. The one who is striving for social progress regards it as a dam through which that progress can only filter or is even blocked altogether. All these men, however, come from a different world and they either consciously or unconsciously have an imperialistic or ethnocentric desire to clean up these peasant rites and to inject into them a different content or at least what seems to them to be a more appropriate symbolism.

We should not forget that the main justification of the feast of a people is to reveal that people's social dimension. A people is fashioned first and foremost by its language and only secondarily by its feasts and its religion. Both, however, are bastions of its identity which has, in this case, been courageously preserved, by resistance, despite three centuries of colonialism and a century and a half of urban or industrial domination. Clinging to these rites is above all the consequence of being oppressed or repressed and the feast somehow expresses this in the form of a symbolic story.

There are only two ways of overcoming the uneasiness caused by this exotic (and therefore pagan) phenomenon which are justifiable methodologically. The first is to take the peasant culture and its rural economy as one's point of departure. In this particular case, this would be Indian society considered not only as a culture, but also—and above all—as a people with a peasant economy and a plan to resist or to express Messianic policies. The rites of the peasants' feast are, after all, the product of that Indian society. The second point of departure is the language of the people, which means that we have to try to decode objectively the semiotic expression of this ritual arrangement. I shall try now to show that this second approach provides us with the keys to open the door to the first.[3]

5. THE SOCIAL MESSAGE OF THE PEASANTS' FEAST

The objects, places, times, rites and people are, as we have seen at the end of the previous section, carefully arranged by the semiotic apparatus of the feast. The liturgy of the feast can also be interpreted as a social 'text' because of its linguistic structure, although the vocabulary, grammar and syntax have first to be understood.

A strange text has also to be translated, in other words, it has to be, in a sense, decoded and encoded, before it can be fully understood. It is necessary to transfer from the register of the language of one culture to that of the other. It is, however, not enough to do this. In order to understand completely, we have to place ourselves in the universe in which that language has become an expression and a communication; in which it has, in other words, become the system of thought resulting from a certain social system. The underground railway, for example, is not only a means of transport, but also a link and an obstacle between places of work and residential areas. It is also an essentially urban phenomenon and at once calls to mind an image of crowding and hustle. If, however, I have never experienced the underground railway, it would be useless for me to translate the term without at the same time situating it within its social context, since only this can reveal its full meaning to me. What would the term 'underground railway' mean, even if it were translated into his language, to a peasant who had never been to the city?

The marginalised peasant's struggle to subsist presupposes a similar approach on the part of the urban spectator at our feasts. If the feast is really, to use Marcel Mauss' phrase, a 'total social phenomenon', it must in some way or other go back to every level of social practice. In the semiotic simulacrum of the latter, peasant rites can only be understood on the basis of the everyday experience of failure in peasant life, of their powerlessness in the struggle to subsist and of their disadvantage with regard to the urban administration which plans their fate. In other words, we can only understand the feast celebrated by the village if we grasp its relationship with the power of the city. This is very difficult for the city-dweller to understand—as difficult for him as the word and the reality 'underground railway' is for the villager.

The whole problem is far too extended for us to consider it in detail here, but we can distinguish the content and the concrete semantic importance of the peasants' feast[4] if we are careful to avoid all urban ideological projections. (These would include hidden forms of syncretism, memories of pre-Christian religious practices and ideas, the artificial selection of values that are open to Christianisation and so on.)

When the village people gather together at the feast of their patron saint, all that this means is that the statue of the saint is the symbol in which they recognise themselves. The gestures, rites and procedure of the feast all reinforce this social message: 'This village is our territory. We have our roots here. We shall never be city-dwellers. Our ancestors are buried here. We want to live and die here.' Sometimes several statues are brought together in a shared feast, in which case the message is: 'We come from the neighbouring village and we have come with the statues of our saints to visit and greet the patron saint of this village. We all need each other. We have to strengthen our bonds with each other because of pressure from the city. Come and see how united we are!'

If the Christian missionary misses the feast, he is at once a stranger, rejecting the opportunity to identify himself with this territory, refusing to become one with this people and placing himself between brackets in the social 'text' or context.

Pine needles are spread over the floor of the church. Seated in a dark corner, the musicans play incessantly. A peasant family comes in and goes to the statue of the saint of the family. They kneel or squat down, putting down their bottle of spirits, the money for their alms or their offering of maize. They light candles and, often with the help of a professional, incant long prayers, frequently weeping. There is a pause, during which they speak freely, as though they were at home. The cup-bearer then pours out a libation of alcohol for every member of the family—men, women and even children at the breast. The incantation is resumed and the candles burn lower. When the maize is offered, the statue and those present are symbolically fondled. The same happens with the offering of the incense.

There is no desecration of the sanctuary, no insult to the sacrament, no theological distortion of the powers of the saint and no heterodoxy in this feast. All that this semiotic simulacrum says is: 'I am poor', although this statement can be made in many different ways: 'The harvest was bad', for example, or 'Hunger has knocked on my door', 'My breasts are living skeletons', 'Good health is not for us', 'Our whole existence is threatened' or 'Death lives among us'.

This message contains no dogmatic deviation. The attempt at syncretism can find no point at which to enter. It is quite respectable. As G. Giménez has pointed out, 'it has simply become a semiotic simulacrum of the processes of real life'. There is no reference to the afterlife in these rites. They point only to the here and now of peasant life and proclaim the marginalisation and exploitation of their existence. What underlies these expressions is not a theological structure, but the everyday economic life of peasant self-subsistence in the country where the ecology has been almost destroyed by the fierce appetite of the city. The imbalance does not have a dogmatic origin. It is a social scandal.

Let us now briefly summarise what the language of the feast of a people does in these rites. Firstly, it affirms the people's identity, territory, history, roots and economy. Secondly, it points to that people's solidarity with other peasants and stresses the ethnical or class bonds between them, because it is clear that the only real power that the peasantry has is its demographic size and the economic pressure that it can exert as a work-force. Thirdly, it defines the people as being poor and exploited and shows that they are always threatened by the power of the city.

There is no reason, apart from the need to concentrate everything in the city, to reject this message and this claim. It could, on the contrary, be a good loophole by which the liturgy can be approached in spirit and in truth. It may, after all, be the form of worship 'that I choose: to loose the bonds of wickedness, to undo the thongs of the yoke, to let the oppressed go free and to break every yoke . . . to share your bread with the hungry?' (Isa. 58:6-7).

6. FLOWERING RIFLES

The great feast, however, is not the village feast. The peasant peoples, who have fought for their dignity as human beings, have regained their land and have seized power, have already been celebrating the real feast for several days without incense, without prostrating themselves and without statues of the saints. They have been singing, beating drums and dancing and, in addition, rifles have played a part in the feast. Just as the Indian peoples take their revenge for being prevented from using powder—the raw material of death for the conquistadores—and transform it into fireworks, so too do the liberated peoples raise rifles decorated with flowers (compare the case of Portugal) because they are no longer used to kill in celebration of their martyrs. In the long struggle for liberation, the regional character of the village was lost. The peasant peoples—about thirty different groups—began to celebrate in this way, in huge popular gatherings accompanied by great merry-making, in the course of the present century. The last peasant population to join in this practice was Nicaragua.

Without losing their ethnic identity, Vietnamese, Indians, Arabs and many black peoples have broken through the colonial tribal barriers. 'In their own languages', as at Pentecost, and in the brotherhood of companions in arms, 'races, peoples and tribes' have overcome the Babel of colonial domination and have acquired the identity of new men. The social change that they have brought about and are celebrating in their feast is not the village holocaust. They have simply gone beyond the village feast. In no case has their feast given way to the values of the western industrial city and to those of the consumer society of the First World pattern. On the contrary, in protesting on behalf of and struggling 'on the side of a humiliated people' and in overthrowing the modern pharaohs, these peoples have rejected the imbalance between the capitalist city and the village and have begun to solve one of the great problems of mankind—that of hunger. Those who produce the food have fiercely rejected the system according to which their land continues to be the larder for the cities of the First World and they are beginning to build a peasant society that is free of hunger and domination.

During the great feast of peoples—the national, not the village feast—hunger, like the beast of the Apocalypse, revealed its presence because the price that had to be paid for the struggle was often to neglect the crops and the cattle. It did not, however, appear as a threatening monster; it was rather seen in its death agony. Instead of killing the fatted calf—or the pig, as they used to for the village feast—these peoples have mobilised their forces to build up a society in which it is no longer a privilege to have a well provided table. Now they are able to transform this dream into a concrete plan. They have thrown open the doors of the imperialist prisons, clothed the prisoners, let those who have hitherto been gagged speak freely and given to everyone the hope of being able to eat with dignity (see Isa. 58:6-7). In so doing, they have given birth to the new man whom they consecrate in their feast of liberation. This is a kind of extraordinary initiation or impressive baptism, after which no one stays the same as he was before. The old man—the oppressed man—has been buried. He died in the street fighting, in the jungle hideouts and the scrubland of the sierra. From now on, there is hope and it is the time of the great feast. This great feast points to a festive daily life of building up a new world. The new rite will be more testing and more demanding than the old one.

Translated by David Smith

Notes

1. The opinions expressed in this section are statements of a choice (a commitment), a conviction (which is publicly confessed here) and a fact of history (studied by specialists). For the historical rôle of the Third World and its essentially peasant character, see Franz Fanon *Les Damnés de la Terre* (Paris 1961); for the connection between the peasant world and the struggles for freedom, see Erik Wolf *The Peasant Wars of the Twentieth Century* (New York 1969); for the peasants' fight against the industrial 'civilisation' of the city, see Pierre Barral *Les Sociétés rurales du XXème siècle* (Paris 1979).

2. Theoretical speculation about this Eucharistic praxis has led to the publication of several essays; for example, 'Un geste risqué; l'eucharistie de Pentecôte 1968, documents et réflexions' *Christianisme Social* (1968), Year 76, Nos. 7-10; Segundo Galilea 'L'eucharistía como protesta' *Vísperas* 21 (1971).

3. The basis for this phenomenology of the feast is, of course, my direct observation of life in the Chiapas villages. My experience of other Indian regions in the sub-continent leads me to assume that all these factors will be encountered, because a structural unity has been slowly built up by the coloniser's jackboot, the imperialist policy, the strategy of the missionaries and the process of achieving independence. The civilisations of the forest-dwellers and the black peoples would have to be described differently, but I believe that the same method and the same concepts as those that I have used here could be applied to these other peoples and would lead to similar conclusions.

4. Apart from the experts in the linguistic and exegetical study of popular narratives (de Saussure, Greimas, Bourdieu, Barthes, etc.), it is particularly valuable to read, in this context, Gilberto Giménez *Cultura Popular y Religión en el Anahuac* (Mexico 1978) pp. 29-54, 197-218, first, because his case study (of the Chalma) has a direct bearing on our attempts to understand the rites described in my article and, second, because he makes an explicit link between the two approaches that I suggest—the linguistic approach ('a semiotic simulacrum of the processes of real life') and the social approach (a ritual dramatisation of the peasant economy of self-subsistence). It is to Giménez that I am indebted for many of the terms used in the article—'cultural (social) text', 'semiotic simulacrum', 'ritual dramatisation' and so on.

Julien Potel

Families and Liturgical Celebrations: Birth, Death and Marriage

TO STUDY the attitudes of families to liturgical celebrations we have chosen three events: birth, death and love and marriage. These are obviously essential in families, so much so that they are often called high points or privileged moments for pastoral work. At such times people are in particular psychological conditions and experience many emotions—not surprisingly, as these events directly involve the forces of life and death. Nevertheless some crucial human activities are less present at these times; examples are work, leisure and political activity.

These three moments, which are moments set apart in family life, are also moments of departure. In a country with an overwhelmingly Christian population baptism, having become almost the monopoly of the churches, helps to integrate the baptised into society as well as being their official introduction into the Church: they are setting out on the Christian life. Religious funerals mark the passage of the deceased to another world: the dead are still 'those who have gone from us' or 'the departed'. For the living this is the beginning of the 'work of mourning' on the psychological level. Marriage, finally, is the entry of the couple into a new social status. To these three moments there correspond 'rites of transition', some of which are then performed for the first or last time.

We are interested primarily in the lives and celebrations of families outside places of worship. The first part of this article looks at the way liturgical celebrations are only stages in much larger complexes of ritual. The second part tackles the complex process of the communication which has to be established between families and representatives of the churches. Many obstacles stand in the way, not least the different centres of interest of the two groups. We find a rich and varied human context: those who prepare and celebrate liturgies should, if possible, take it into account.

1. LITURGIES AS PARTS OF COMPLEXES OF RITUAL

Families celebrating a birth, death or marriage are constructing a complex of individual and collective rituals in which liturgies take their place. The people who come

65

to a place of worship for a baptism have already ritualised the birth and will continue to celebrate it afterwards. They retain a large measure of autonomy in their way of doing so. They will, for example, already have had to choose a name for the child, announce the 'good news' with letters or cards. There are visits in hospital or at home, with flowers and presents. The father may celebrate the birth with his friends with 'a drink or two'. There are also godparents to be chosen, the date for the baptism to be fixed, preparations to be made for the celebrations (clothes for the child, a special meal and food rituals). The godparents and friends may bring gifts. After the baptism there are annual birthday celebrations.

The ritual complex surrounding funerals is more of a piece, but in the industrialised countries families are subject to social constraints which curb their initiatives. The hospital, the State and the undertakers intervene and impose rules. In one sense, the family is dispossessed of the death of a member of the family and is tightly guided in its funeral rites. However, various rites surround the Christian ceremony: notices of decease, in language which changes with time, the attention given to the funeral, and in particular to the quality and beauty of the coffin, visits to the family or the mortuary chapel, the wake, the coffining, mourning clothes or emblems, flowers and wreaths, burial in the cemetery and mementoes for the grave, the funeral meal, souvenir photos of the deceased, anniversaries of his or her death.

The ritualisation of love around religious marriage is also becoming more elaborate. Here families really retain the initiative. They choose the date of the ceremony and announce it by means of formal notices. The young man 'buries his bachelor life'; usually libations with friends celebrate his forthcoming transition to the status of husband. Collections are organised, especially at work, for presents and the couple guides the choice with lists. Invitations are issued to those who will make up the 'wedding party'. Various old customs survive: special wedding clothes and a procession, especially in the country, decoration of cars and houses. Then comes the civil marriage ceremony (at least in such countries as France). After the liturgy there is the reception with its food rituals, dances, songs and music. Photos of the marriage taken by a professional photographer will be distributed to the guests and some will finally be displayed in the houses. Finally rituals connected with the wedding night and the day following the wedding also persist. Later come the wedding anniversaries: tin, silver, gold.

These three significant moments are used by certain families, consciously or unconsciously, for an outward affirmation of their position in society, their power or wealth. Ostentatious behaviour ensures or reinforces their social prestige, particularly at the times of marriages and funerals. Baptisms, which do not attract a large attendance and have no processions, give little opportunity for such behaviour. At funerals, however, families can very easily celebrate themselves by an outward display. Some give themselves a pat on the back: 'We gave him a good send-off'; 'He had a lovely service and a beautiful coffin'. In the words of a French novelist writing in 1928 about the French peasantry, 'The price of the coffin, the class of the service and later the stone and the bordering of the grave, and the flowers grown there are all so many posthumous obligations which involve family honour and are watched with a jealous eye by the neighbours.' In Nagisa Oshima's film The Ceremony the main hero, Masuo, says after his mother's funeral: 'It was huge. People said that my grandfather had paid for his own funeral in his lifetime.' But marriages give more encouragement to display. The beauty and display of the clothes, the organisation of the procession, the decorations, the quality of the meal and the number of guests, the search for a 'beautiful service' at the church—especially if any civil ceremony is unspectacular—the lavishness, excess and extravagance inherent in the celebration, establish and raise the family in the eyes of others.

This aspect is encouraged by the effect of economic and social contexts on families. In developed industrial societies the massive production and consumption, the media and advertising, form an environment which invites the organisers of celebrations to multiply expenditure, the number of gifts and other transactions. Without necessarily creating needs, this environment may stimulate the buying and selling mechanism in the organisers. It offers mental models which encourage expenditure or certain ways of celebrating. Birth and christening, for example, are objects of advertising. There are shops with clothes specially designed for mothers-to-be and their babies. There are firms specialising in receptions, buffets and cakes. Magazine reports feature certain baptisms in royal families or the world of show business. Funerals, however, loom larger than baptisms in the world of customers for liturgy. The making of money out of death has often been denounced. The dead person becomes 'the loved one'. He is genuinely missed, but his funeral is expensive. The mass production and mass consumption society exploits people in grief and mourning. The place of funerals in the media deserves lengthy discussion, but here we may simply note the treatment of the funerals of film and show business figures, politicians and religious leaders, or ordinary people killed in dramatic circumstances. Some civil or religious funerals become political issues. They turn into meetings, sometimes even into battles which bring opposing forces into conflict. Everyone remembers the funeral of Mgr Romero, the Archbishop of San Salvador, in March 1980, which was turned into a murderous gun battle.

Marriages seem to take pride of place in the socio-economic environment of customers for ceremonies. There is no lack of advertising for wedding dresses and other wedding clothes, gifts, receptions and buffets; a section of the press specialises in this area. Engaged couples are a potential market, and receive the attentions of manufacturers of household equipment. In addition the media run features on royal weddings, and the happy or stormy relationships of certain stars are described or dramatised.

The individual and collective rituals which mark birth, marriage and death are, then, many and varied. The liturgical celebrations are only a part of them. Not all these rituals have the same significance and their religious density varies. Families participate in them with greater or lesser intensity. They may get more involved in rituals in which they retain the initiative than in those offered to them by the churches in the course of the liturgical celebrations.

2. THE NECESSARY BUT DIFFICULT TASK OF COMMUNICATION

Preparation for liturgies and ceremonies gives pastoral workers an opportunity for contact with the families. According to circumstances, the complex process of communication succeeds to a greater or lesser extent. Obstacles do arise, but there are also ways of encouraging the process.

(a) Triangular or bipolar relations?

In baptism three parties are present: the baby, its family and the full-time religious functionaries. However, only two enter into communication, the parents and the religious functionaries. The babies are outside since, by definition, the infant remains the *infans*, the one who does not speak. In fact, he or she is the person principally concerned in the baptism. The celebrant's words and the meaning of the rites are in theory communicated to all except the principal beneficiary. At first it looked as though there was a triangular relation between the three parties involved, but in fact the human communication is no more than bipolar, between the religious functionaries and the parents, who are indirectly concerned in the baptism in which they are taking part.

Certain features of celebrations of baptism may also be a source of difficulty. I do not mean the symbolism inherent in the liturgy, which is not always intelligible to people today, or the strangeness of the changes to some people. I am thinking of more practical things. The parents very often think of a baptism 'for them', on a date they have chosen, when only their child will be baptised. The spread of collective baptisms, especially in towns, with dates fixed in advance, may create difficulties, and some priests also advise parents not to let a day go by before contacting them. For the families the place of the god-parents is psychologically important on the day of the baptism, but in the liturgy it takes second place to that of the parents. In the same way preparation meetings are increasingly suggested to parents and they approach the liturgy in a new state of mind. The other participants in the baptism ceremony, however, have not taken part in the preparation: the audience is not homogeneous. Finally, some of the participants capture the baptism in photos or on film and this becomes the memory, while the date itself is pushed out of mind by that of the birth. It is sometimes annoying to see photographers in action during the ceremony. Some seem more anxious to get good shots than to take a real part in the ceremony.

Being realistic about the attitudes of parents at the birth of a baby may improve communications. It is wrong to idealise birth by regarding it as nothing but a source of joy. Of course joys exist, but some births are awaited and experienced in anguish and loneliness. And the arrival of a child always brings worries: for its health and that of the mother, how far its arrival is wanted and accepted, worries about the future, about its reception by brothers and sisters. For parents a birth brings new responsibilities and changes in their relationship as a couple and with others. When they come for a baptism they are going through all that, in one way or another.

It is difficult to make the point without a joke, but it is a fact that at religious funerals too the main beneficiary says nothing. The celebrant's words do not reach him or her. The only communication established is with the participants who are the indirect objects of the ceremony. This inability of the person principally concerned to express himself or to participate creates imbalances in communication at baptisms and funerals. On pastoral grounds it is necessary to direct the message to people who are the indirect beneficiaries, though without forgetting the direct beneficiaries of the celebration, who take no part.

Remembering some reactions of families at funerals may also ease communications in a situation where, in contrast with baptism, it is impossible to have a period of preparation. While it may be a commonplace to remark that the celebrant is meeting people who are physically and emotionally exhausted, the fact still has important consequences for the celebration. When grief is great everyone spontaneously seeks silence, and this explains the common difficulty of getting active participation and sustained attention. Families are destroyed by the brutal and unexpected breaking of the bonds which previously united them visibly with the deceased. The confusion must be made worse by the denial of death which is epidemic in highly industrialised societies. Death is not accepted for what it is, but hidden. Again, since material and earthly happiness are more and more held up as goals, death becomes even more of a failure and an absurdity which creates revolt and disgust. Mourning may sometimes become the time for asking 'Why?', and death the ultimate question about the meaning of existence. Some relatives may feel guilt towards the dead person and blame themselves for not having paid him or her enough attention. Finally, divisions may separate the members of the family, whether or not they attend the ceremony. 'Family quarrels' in the past, and rivalries and jealousies about legacies, are real. Death may be an opportunity for the members of the family to forget what used to keep them apart, to go beyond them, in short, to forgive each other. There is a sense in which the dead confront the living with questions.

In contrast to a baptism or a funeral, in a marriage the representatives of the churches are in direct communication with the main beneficiaries of the liturgy. The family stays in second place. Communication is bipolar, directly with those who ask for the ceremony, who are at the same time the people principally involved. As a result, at the beginning of the liturgical celebration there may be a gap between the state of mind of the couple and that of the relatives and guests. The couple have had discussions with the priests or the Christians responsible for preparation, and changes in attitude often take place. The relatives and guests have not been through this process.

For better communication with engaged couples it is important to remember that the wedding day follows a long period of preparation. Young people will have known each other for years. In all cases the day will have been looked forward to and talked about in detail beforehand. The practical details of setting up house are further worries added to the organisation of the wedding. Psychologically all this often takes precedence over preparation for the religious ceremony. As with a birth, realism about the situation is essential. Normally, indeed, the discovery of love is accompanied by a dynamic joy, but married lives can also get off to a difficult start. Marriage is also a break with the family, which does not always accept this and may not relax its embrace, and a break with old habits as a result of the transition to the status of a married couple. Nowadays premarital cohabitation is increasingly frequent. In France, out of a sample of 270 married couples questioned between 1976 and the beginning of 1977, 44 per cent had lived together before marriage. For the two previous years the proportion had been 37 per cent. This new situation is a sign of a change in ways of seeing love and marriage. A final difficulty in the dialogue between families and the representatives of the churches has to do with the actual nature of the area of human activity involved. Symbols of love and sex and references to it may be interpreted in different ways. They are riddled with hidden implications and double entendres. It is a subject in which laughs, jokes and sniggers come easily, as the reactions of some guests at marriage ceremonies prove.

(b) Differences of expectation and aim among the participants

In relationships between the families and the representatives of the churches during the three periods under discussion the expectations and assumptions, the centres of interest and aims of the participants are not the same. The families' reasons for wanting a ceremony, whether they realise it or not, do not always coincide with the perspectives put forward or the aims pursued by the religious representatives. The following attempt to contrast the positions of families and priests is of course not an appeal for pastoral work to be adapted to the habits of families. The representatives of the churches have to cope with the convergences and divergences which exist between the families and themselves.

According to a survey, those who ask for a baptism for small children regard it as an almost absolute right. The religious functionary may not refuse it and they have a right to receive it more or less without difficulty. This is why from the outset some demands made by the clergy are not always understood. Again, the parents come for their child, which is the whole reason for and point of their action. They are thinking first and foremost of the child. In the preparation and pastoral work, however, the religious workers concentrate on the parents and invite them to think about the meaning of their request and the meaning of their lives and beliefs. The parents tend also to be more concerned with immediate problems: the arrangements for the christening, the choice of the god-parents, worries about the family get-together. While they do not forget the present, the representatives of the churches are more aware of the period after baptism, with its future demands. They insist on the 'consequential' aspect of baptism. And of course for the parents it remains a family event. The priests regard it as such, of course, but they also see it as a hope for the local and even the universal Church, in which the person to be baptised is expected to fulfil the promises of his baptism.

Similarly, at religious funerals relatives and representatives of the Church do not emphasise the same things. The families are celebrating the memory of someone belonging to them; the memories they retain of the person tend to concentrate on the praiseworthy side of his or her life and the shadows fade into the background. The liturgy certainly takes account of the good done by the dead person, but prayers are offered also for someone who has sinned before God and men. For the participants, too, the liturgy is primarily a family affair, on a small scale, whereas the liturgy itself brings in the universal Church far beyond the small group of mourning relatives. Lastly, at a funeral families are celebrating their human condition. The death of another person forces them to consider the mystery of their death. The rites become a way of giving themselves security, of exorcising and banishing death.

The difference in perspective also complicates communication between the religious functionaries and the couple at religious weddings. For many couples love and especially sexual life are still a strictly private area which concerns no one but them and certainly not celibate and childless priests. In contrast to the situation in baptism and funerals, the people who have requested the ceremony are here directly and intimately involved in their action. The privatisation of religion does not make discussion easier. An attempt to touch on certain topics, or a public reference to the life of the couple before marriage, may seem like an attempt to interfere in a carefully guarded area. There are also differences of view about the family, relations between men and women, civil marriage and the sacrament of marriage. For example, what significance do the couple and the representatives of the churches attach to civil marriage? Various contemporary situations also produce gulfs which hinder communication. Hesitation about a binding commitment, the frequency of premarital cohabitation, attitudes to abortion and the place of children, the increase in divorces and the climate of eroticism, all these are matters on which the couple and the representatives of the churches may not necessarily agree.

At the three moments of family life we have chosen, there are signs in some areas or some countries of a loss of vitality in Catholicism and rejections of belief. These appear at several levels. First there is that of religious practice: figures for baptisms are dropping and the gaps between birth and baptism are increasing. The Catholic liturgy of the dead seems to be holding up better, but here, too, we occasionally find a drop in the number of funeral Masses. Some of the figures for religious marriages are also falling and the services are being reduced to 'simple blessings' without a Mass.

At the level of beliefs held, some of those who ask for ceremonies staunchly affirm their total rejection of the faith and display a lack of interest in it. In the case of baptism, for example, acceptance of the reality of sin and in particular of personal conversion has weakened. What beliefs about eternal life and the resurrection are held by the participants in Christian funerals? Who is the risen Jesus for them? What has he to do with the dead member of their family and their mourning? In the area of everyday behaviour there is a greater or lesser degree of harmony between the conduct of those who ask for services and the assumptions or the morality of the churches. Contact with engaged couples is one way of verifying this.

Much of the difficulty in communication between those who come to ask for a ceremony and the religious functionaries can be explained by the difference in social status between the two sides. The official representatives of a religious institution (which also has social dimensions) have the power of performing Christian worship, the power to admit someone to a religious ceremony and to celebrate it. In the three moments under discussion another factor is the status of the childless celibate priest who has to deal with couples who have had children or who are about to do so. Even if the priest is a member of a family, even if his everyday ministry has given him an intimate knowledge of the lives of families, he remains excluded from a direct and extended experience of the joys, worries and responsibilities of the father of a family. In addition those who seek liturgical celebrations are placed within the context and the movement of a celebration which, as we have seen, is wider than the Christian celebration. They have the status of people engaged in celebration, even at a funeral. The celebrant enters into the celebration for a moment, but he is not one of the 'christening party' or the 'wedding party', with all the festive implications of those terms.

The status of families and couples who come for a baptism, a wedding or a funeral is that of applicants. They are taking an initiative to obtain a religious ceremony. From the start their position includes an element of dependence on the religious functionaries, and their reactions to the Church as an institution play a part. Some will be embarrassed, tense or feel guilty because they have moved away from the Church. A minority may even have some disagreement to settle and will be aggressive and closed. They are re-entering the 'Catholic world' they have abandoned or rejected. They are no longer at home there.

The idea each person has of the other also plays a role in communication. In the eyes of non-practising applicants—sometimes the majority—the representative of the Church is the man who knows, who knows how to speak and 'knows his way around'. But any communication demands an attitude of strong and shared confidence.

The representatives of the Church and the applicants do not start off on the same footing. Many take the initiative in making a request for the specific purpose of obtaining a celebration. They seek out the priest because of his particular competence and because of the religious power he exercises. It is a social relationship of a particular type known as a 'functional relationship', comparable with that of a patient consulting a doctor for his competence and powers. The essence of the pastoral attitude lies in recognising the different status of the applicants and then in making the initial relationship develop into a confident, personal communicaiton which is demanding but mutually enriching.

Translated by Francis McDonagh

F

Adalbert de Vogüé

Monastic Life and Times of Prayer in Common

UNTIL recently the way monks discharged choral office conformed more than anything else they did to the prescriptions of St Benedict. Each monastery in principle celebrated seven offices through the day and a night office as the Rule[1] envisaged. This daily cycle had, however, undergone various modifications down the ages. Thus, for example, the office of prime had come to include the little chapter and a conventual Mass was said in the morning after one of the little hours, whilst certain orders recited a supplementary office of Our Lady after the normal hours. Besides these additions, many liberties were taken with the horary: offices celebrated at an hour different from the one for which they had been designed[2] or recited one after the other.[3] This last practice reduced the number of celebrations with a distinctive character of their own. The recitation of three or four hours on the trot meant that one was no longer praising God 'seven times a day' as St Benedict had provided, but much less.

These practices were no less shocking for having been duly ratified by indults and the rubrics, and many monasteries set about reforming them courageously at the beginning of this century. Each office was detached from its neighbouring office and celebrated for itself, at its own time.[4] This striving for truth involved certain sacrifices and very naturally it tended to bring in its train a suppression of additions to the normal hours. Whereas the conventual Mass remained part of every timetable, the office of Our Lady disappeared, as did too the chapter prayers at prime. But with the reform of Vatican II this tendency went well beyond a simple return to the Rule of St Benedict. Thus the latter had prescribed the office of prime, and yet it has for the most part been dropped. There are places where the office preceding Mass is left out, and where one or other of the little hours is said only in private. It has even been suggested that St Benedict's sevenfold scheme should be reduced to a threefold one—and this proposal has sometimes been carried through.

1. UNCEASING PRAYER

We need to test this very varied and shifting situation against the deep and permanent exigencies of the monastic life. Is it possible, in the light of the origins of monasticism, to discern the basic meaning of the prayer of the hours, the place it should hold in practice, the forms which validate it, and the risks it runs? We put these questions not in any spirit of mere historical curiosity but in order to shed light on the choices which people make today. They amount to asking what people today who feel drawn to be monks can get out of this tradition of prayer in common going back to late antiquity.

It is not difficult to discern the original sense of the office. Vatican II expressed it well: 'The divine office is arranged so that the whole course of the day and night is made holy by the praises of God'; 'that the day may be truly sanctified', in obedience to the directive of the apostle: 'Pray constantly'.[5] This is indeed the first aim of the traditional cycle and its one and only scriptural root. It is a matter not of producing a certain quantity of prayers said at any moment within the space of twenty-four hours but of the existence of as continual a prayer as possible based on the support of celebrations spaced at regular intervals.

'Pray constantly.' It is impossible to exaggerate the importance of this instruction— the only one given on the subject in the New Testament—because it is based at once on the freedom of the Christian in the face of every system of celebration and on the obligation he is under to choose one such system and then to follow it faithfully. On the one hand, therefore, freedom: neither the Christian nor the monk is bound to any particular rhythm of recourse to God. On the other hand, obligation: they must love the Lord their God with all their heart, that is to say with all their time, and this call to incessant prayer entails effective means of implementation which always tend to befall short of their end and so to pass beyond themselves.

Prayer at certain fixed times is, therefore, only a means towards unceasing prayer. Like any other means it must be adjusted to its end and needs to be perpetually attentive thereto. Like any means, too, it runs the risk of forgetting its proper end and of substituting itself for it. This is what happens as soon as one thinks of the prayer one says at certain moments in terms of having done one's bit so that one does not need to pay any further attention to God. The truth of the matter is that, whatever rhythm one adopts, these discontinuous celebrations always fall infinitely short of an ideal that is in itself limitless since it consists in responding to the Lord's invitation to each one of us to 'pray constantly'.

It follows that if one binds oneself to some definite observance—to pray at such and such an hour—this does not amount to pretending to discharge a limitless debt but to find in this practice support for the infinite effort to which one feels oneself called. The hours of prayer are only the infrastructure of continual prayer, the accented moments in a melody which aspires to be uninterrupted. Their aim is to realise the continuous consecration of time in a figurative and inchoate way. The Christian who observes them finds in them a reminder, staggered over shorter or longer intervals, of his call to pray without ceasing, a safeguard against immersion into temporal anxieties and forgetfulness of the Lord, a renewal of his converse with God.

2. THE THINKING OF THE FATHERS

I have developed these thoughts elsewhere,[6] but they are not just edifying comments for the modern reader. They relay the very way in which the old authors from Tertullian onwards tackled this question. In a page of his *De oratione*,[7] which is echoed exactly by Cyprian, Jerome, Augustine and Cassian, the Carthaginian priest crystallised what will become common doctrine: the only rule Christ left about the times of prayer was to 'pray constantly'. At the same time it is not useless to establish certain definite times for oneself in order to give concrete expression to the Lord's call and to wrench oneself more firmly away from one's preoccupations. The most appropriate hours are the third, the sixth and the ninth since they punctuate the secular day[8] and Scripture mentions them. This celebration of the three main hours of the day is optional and breaks up the lapse of time between the two big and obligatory moments constituted by the beginning of the day and the beginning of the night.

Compared with this luminous teaching, St Benedict's presentation of the cycle of the hours seems to represent a simplification. It is not just that their number increases from five to eight. The essential thing is that their more or less optional character ceases to be noted. St Benedict thinks of the seven day hours as being required in a uniform way by the words of the psalmist, 'Seven times a day I praise thee', just as he also thinks of the night office as being required by another text of the psalms.[9] Three centuries of development have issued in an absolute canonisation of the 'sacred sevenfold'. It is no longer referred back to the 'pray constantly' any more than it takes account of the distinction between the necessary and the free. This late presentation is summary and inadequate and so obviously calls for a return to the source represented by the *De oratione* of the third century and to the New Testament root so well exposed by Tertullian.

Between this latter and St Benedict, however, Christians engaged in a long process of reflection about the 'Pray constantly', and out of this meditation produced certain hermeneutic principles, some of which have come back into favour. Whereas the Messalians derived a condemnation of work and a programme of purely spiritual work out of this Pauline directive, other teachers on the contrary interpreted it as a simple invitation to pray from time to time and to act well in the meantime. The modern slogan 'Work is prayer' roughly sums up the substance of these interpretations made by masters as eminent as Origen, Aphraates and Augustine.

If one goes along with several recent authors and accepts such views even to the point of pressing them upon monks themselves,[10] one is identifying with the idea we had set aside a little earlier: that of the sufficiency of the hours of the office. On such a view they would amount to a sum of prayers which would be the end of the matter. This was, however, not the way the ancients thought of things. When Cassian declares that the 'whole aim of the monk is to tend towards uninterrupted prayer'[11] he is doing no more than express a generally held view. Neither St Basil, nor even St Augustine, think otherwise.[12] All agree that the monk can pass no moment, not even his time of work, without striving to talk with God by means of the ceaseless recitation of the scriptural word,[13] which calls upon him to respond to the Lord with brief and frequent prayers. However we set about working towards this ideal—and we moderns with our atrophied memories can always resort to a mantra[14]—no monk worthy of the name can give up the intention to fill his whole time, between the offices, with waiting upon God and in true prayer.

3. THE COURSE OF OFFICES

It is by reference to this personal intention to engage in ceaseless prayer that we have to appreciate any particular *cursus* or sequence of community offices. Their object is to sustain every monk in his effort, not to dispense him from it or to disgust him with it. They are like the pillars of a bridge the only purpose of which is to support the roadway. What is the use of sinking these pillars if one does not use them to form the bridge which joins the two banks and enables one to pass from one to another without let? Gatherings for prayer at given moments are only such pillars designed to support unceasing prayer. Their number does not matter provided they do in fact carry the continuous work which they are meant to sustain.

If we apply this criterion to the variation in the number of offices we come to see that these vicissitudes are basically ambiguous. The multiplication of times of prayer, whether permanently or at certain periods, as has been done here and there,[15] does indeed signify a concern to pray a lot, but it also signifies a loss of confidence in the individual monk's personal and constant application to prayer. Again the diminution of prayer in common can come about, as it did in Egypt and Syria in the fourth century,[16] because each individual monk gives himself up to scriptural 'meditation' and prayer the whole day long, but it can also come about because one wants to make more time for temporal activities carried on, as Tertullian had already feared, without any real effort to attend to God, let alone without any serious possibility of recollection. In the latter case, which has occurred many a time during the recent *aggiornamento*, the abandonment of certain hours of the office represents the loss of the religious spirit, a slide towards secularisation.

It would, therefore, be illusory to give a general and theoretical answer to the question: 'Does the office attain its objective of hallowing the monk's day?' The true reply depends on what each and all do, not only with the time passed in choir, but with the time in between. The hours of prayer in common are useful and necessary in proportion to the degree to which the existence which they punctuate is consecrated to the effective search for God, that is to say, to an effort of constant prayer permeating all one's activities. If it is, the office becomes less indispensable. If it is not, the office resumes all its importance as a reminder and stimulus of constant prayer.

In practice, in the activist and secularising world in which we live, the Benedictine *cursus* of the seven hours is a good test of the monastic quality of any community. The readiness to let oneself be disturbed regularly and frequently by the office seems to be a touchstone of the authenticity of a group of monks nowadays, just as it constituted a criterion of the individual vocation in the eyes of St Benedict.[17] It is, however, such a sign of monastic health only in the polluted atmosphere of our age of materialism and the death of God. But let us envisage an existence entirely devoted to converse with God, as one finds it in certain hermitages in America. A monk who lives there can dispense himself without harm from all hours of the office in order to give himself up to his unceasing work in full liberty. This is what the Scetiotes of the fifth century did, whose way of life John of Gaza opposed to that of the cenobites: in contrast with the hours and the songs of the latter, a continual 'meditation' shot through with rapid prayers of the lips accompanied manual work.[18]

It is between these two extremes—the monk who does not pray outside of choir and the one who prays ceaselessly as well as or even better than he does in choir—that the choral office deploys the whole range of possibilities of help. It is for each person to choose, in the truth of his existence, the method best suited to support his effort of continual presence to God. We must, however, fill out this general maxim with a few more particular remarks on precise points which condition the eminently practical enterprise that is the sanctification of the day by times of prayer.

4. THE HORARY

The first question is about the horary. The horary indicated by St Benedict is both determined by ancient usage and yet very free in their regard. What antiquity bequeathed to him was the reference to the solar system (dawn, the rising and setting of the sun, and the fall of the night) and the division of the day into four equal portions into which Christian asceticism, following certain indications in the Scriptures, inserted the prayers of terce, sext and none. What St Benedict allowed himself to modify was the precise hour of each celebration, which he put forward or back slightly, with an unsual freedom, to suit the convenience of work and the *lectio divina*.[19]

Nowadays such a horary confronts us with a fundamental problem: What is the significance of such a division of the day which no longer corresponds to the structure of secular life as we have it? One is tempted to replace it with a *cursus* based on the rhythm of human life as we really lead it. Without rejecting such a proposal *a priori*, we should note the permanent interest represented in the traditional series of little hours by the fact that they punctuate the day regularly by expressing the desire not to leave any substantial period of time without prayer. And as for the reference to the sun, it preserves such a power of suggestive and religious symbolism that, far from eliminating it, one would like to see it restored and revalued. Fortunate are those who can regulate their existence according to these great cosmic phenomena, with their seasonal variations, and in this way to escape from the imprisonment of modern man in a uniform and abstract time under an artificial, unvarying and bleak light.

At the same time, the system of solar hours was not the only one elaborated by tradition. After recommending the five hours, Tertullian goes on to enumerate many other occasions on which it was also suitable to pray.[20] Such indications are still sporadic in Tertullian, but under Ambrose's pen they become organised into another scheme (waking, leaving the house, beginning and end of the meal, the hour of incense, sleep), in which the sun's course remained the backdrop but which takes as its explicit guiding thread human activities. A similar tendency is observable in St Benedict: he keeps the names of the little hours, but in fact he places these offices at the beginning or the end of the monks' activities. These adaptations are suggestive in a time such as ours when the demand for effective work is so strong. They open the way to intelligent combinations of the criterion of the hours and that of activities in the interest of a realistic life of prayer.

Another point that needs to be registered is the interest that the celebration of determined hours has even in the case of a more or less constant prayer which would seem to make offices almost irrelevant. Even in such a hypothesis, says St Basil, one should not neglect gatherings for prayer in common, because such gatherings commemorate in a special way the particular benefits of God.[21] This memory of biblical events is a constant characteristic of the ancient *cursus*. What St Basil adds to this is motivations borrowed from the needs of the spiritual life, which take on different shapes at different moments of the day.[22] More generally, we should emphasise that an almost continual attention to God is not incompatible with deriving benefit from more intense and more exclusive moments of attention.[23]

5. MASS

We need to make a final remark about the Mass. We should not allow the undeniable progress represented by concelebration to obscure the fact that the Mass remains heterogeneous to the *cursus* of the office in so far as it has no necessary relationship either with the day nor with the hours. Its daily and solemn celebration poses a problem which can be resolved only by a progressive transformation of mentalities. A decisive step would be to gain a better understanding of the meaning and value of primitive Eucharistic customs: the Mass reserved for Sunday—for the greater glory both of the Sunday and of the Mass—and a simple service of communion on weekdays.

To conclude, I should like to note at least one of the gaps in this article. From beginning to end I have advisedly mingled two questions: that of the times of prayer and that of times of prayer said *in common*. These questions are nevertheless distinct: the first arises even for a solitary monk, whilst the second specifically concerns cenobites. The latter have to ask themselves not only what rhythm of life is most conducive to their personal unfolding, but also how the intention to pray ceaselessly will express itself effectively at the community level. We cannot here deal with this last theme which would lead us to consider—in order to set aside—the example of the Acoemetae and of the *Laus perennis*. Honesty, however, obliges us at least to say that we ought to deal with it.

Translated by John Maxwell

Notes

1. Referred to hereafter as *RB*. See *RB* 16, 1-5.
2. In order to throw the conventual Mass in the middle of the morning into greater relief those involved in the restoration of the nineteenth-century displaced sext and none on those days when they were meant to precede the Mass. See J. Dubois 'Office des heures et messe dans la tradition monastique' *La Maison-Dieu* 135 (1978) 61-82, at 80.
3. See already *Ordo Romanus* 12, 22 (terce, sext, none) in M. Andrieu *Les Ordines Romani* II (Louvain 1948) p. 464.
4. Except, for the most part, the offices of vigils and matins (see *RB* 8, 4).
5. *Constitution on the Liturgy* §§ 84, 86 (1 Thess. 5:17) 88, 94.
6. *La Règle de saint Benoît* VII (Paris 1977) pp. 184-205.
7. Tertullian *Or.* 24-26. See Cyprian *Dom. or.* 34-36; Jerome *Ep.* 22, 37; Augustine *Ep.* 130, 18; Cassian *Instit.* 3, 3, 8.
8. See also Tertullian *De ieiunio* 10, 3.
9. *RB* 16, 1-5, quoting Ps. 118, 164; 118, 62.
10. See *La Règle de saint Benoît* VII pp. 222-240.
11. Cassian *Coll.* 9, 2, 1.
12. Basil *Reg. fus.* 37, 2-3; Augustine *Mor. Eccl.* 1, 67 and *Op. mon.* 20.
13. This practice is akin to the *psalterium currens* and to the *lectio continua* of the Bible in the office. Even work is accompanied by the mutter of meditation.
14. See J. Main in *Cistercian Studies* 12 (1977) 184-190.
15. See *La Règle du Maître* II (Paris 1964) (*SC* 106) p. 239 n. 2.
16. In Egypt work was done to the accompaniment of 'meditation' (Cassian *Instit.* 3, 2 etc.). In Syria they did not work (Theodoret *HR* 2, 5; 4, 5).
17. See *RB* 58, 7: *si sollicitus est ad opus Dei*.
18. *Ep.* 74 (143). There was, however, a celebration of office morning and evening in Scete, as there was already in the time of Cassian *Instit.* 2, 4.
19. *RB* 48. See *La Règle de saint Benoît* V (*SC* 185) pp. 589-604.
20. Tertullian *Or.* 25, 6-26, 2; Ambrose *De uirginibus* 3, 18.
21. Basil *Reg. fus.* 37, 3.
22. In this connection it is instructive to compare *RB* 7, 10-30 and 19, 1-2.
23. See *La Règle de saint Benoît* VII pp. 240-248.

Heinrich Rennings

The Christian Sunday and Special Purpose Sundays

THE TENDENCY to allot a determined theme, a specialised appeal or purpose, to individual Sundays of the year is certainly not wholly new; but it has become considerably stronger in recent times. It is not only a question of giving a Sunday a definite title, but, more seriously, of highlighting in varying degrees the theme of the Sunday concerned liturgically, especially in the celebration of the Sunday Mass. Is such a development pure gain for parishes and their worship, or should one rather be warning them of its dangers?

1. THE PROLIFERATION OF SPECIAL PURPOSE SUNDAYS

In 1926 the Apostolic See, at the request of the general council of the Pontifical Society for the Propagation of the Faith, made the last Sunday in October a 'day of prayer and action for the missions'.[1] In the celebration of the Sunday Mass the sermon and certain supplementary prayers were to bear on this particular cause. At that time it was not yet foreseen that votive Masses for the Propagation of the Faith might actually supplant the Mass of the Sunday. The rescript introducing this *dies pro missionibus* (as it was later called) said nothing about the details of extra-liturgical activities in support of mission.[2] In 1952 Pius XII recommended the celebration of a *dies pro emigrantibus* on the First Sunday of Advent throughout the entire Latin Church. Out of this in 1969 came the annual *dies migratoris*, authorised by an instruction of the Congregation for Bishops.[3] Stimulated by these special days, the Second Vatican Council in its decree *On the Instruments of Social Communication* asked the bishop of every diocese to determine at his own discretion one day each year when the faithful might have their duties in the area of the mass media brought home to them. 'They should be invited to reflect on these questions in prayer and to make financial provision for them.'[4] While mission day was to be simply allocated to its appointed Sunday, the conciliar decree speaks of the 'celebration' of a day of the media, introduced in 1971 under the title *dies mundialis communicationis socialis*.[5] According to the proposals of the papal commission within whose competence this theme belonged, it was to have (to take the single example of 1978) the following rubric: 'those in receipt of social communication— their expectations, their rights, their duties'. Proper Scripture readings were appointed, along with bidding prayers, and a particular Sunday, the Seventh Sunday of Eastertide, was set aside for it. Early in 1964 another theme for intercession was laid down, that of the promotion of vocations to the priesthood and the religious life, and to this was assigned the Sunday whose gospel is that of the Good Shepherd.[6] The Sunday liturgy was to incorporate this theme in a *dies mundialis precum pro vocationibus.*[7] Yet another example of a theme day introduced by Rome is the day of world peace introduced on 1 January for which 'the Apostolic See is to publish annually appropriate suggestions for the theme of the celebration'.[8]

Finally, thematic Sundays in a wider sense also include, at the level of the whole Latin Rite, the Sunday in the Octave of Christmas, the Sunday following Pentecost and the closing Sunday of the Church's year. It is a permanent feature of these Sundays that they mark 'feasts'—the Holy Family, the Holy Trinity, Christ the King—which treat more of a specific theme than they do of the events of salvation history, although it is the latter that really form the basis for Christian festivals.[9] Reservations about such feasts founded on a theological principle or a devotional practice are to be found in the commentary accompanying the promulgation of the General Roman Calendar and should not be overlooked.[10]

In addition to these themes of mission, emigrants, the media, vocations, peace, and Holy Family, Trinity and Christ the King, we now have, at national, diocesan and parochial level, still more numerous thematic Sundays. As special purpose Sundays of this kind, that is, Sundays which subserve a definite religious, ecclesial or social objective, the Swiss Bishops' Conference, for instance, declared the following: Sunday in the world-wide octave of prayer for the reunion of Christendom, Sunday of the sick, day of thanksgiving, repentance and prayer for the Swiss Confederation.[11] Elsewhere we find a Sunday for the protection of the environment, a Sunday of the handicapped, a minorities Sunday.[12] Whoever would dream of forbidding organisations that express the Christian love of neighbour their own Caritas Sunday, or of depriving those concerned with helping Catholics in remote areas of a special Diaspora Sunday![13] The abundant liturgical texts and homiletic notes specially prepared for these occasions show a concern to impress the given Sunday with as strong a mark as possible of the special appeal, and to make it yield as much as possible in special collections. In this way the given Sunday's liturgy is often enough quite overlaid by the special appeal in question.[14]

2. MAKING THE SUNDAY LITURGY A PERTINENT REALITY?

What should we think about the growth of special purpose Sundays? If we disregard the quite understandable, even laudable, ambition of papacy, episcopate and the rest to win a Sunday for causes dear to their hearts, we are left with the impression that the inventors of the special purpose Sunday were barely conscious at all of questions to do with the theology of the liturgy. Yet should we take it for granted that the Sunday liturgy should be mutilated or even suppressed altogether by some special cause? On the one hand we have the existence of some objective deemed to be important (for example, mission); on the other, the insight that this objective concerns all Christians and should occupy them, in intercessory prayer, for example. Between them these two factors ostensibly suffice to create their own 'Sunday'. But in this kind of approach it is impossible to see why more Sundays, indeed why each and every Sunday of the year should not feature an annually recurring theme. After all, there is no lack of good causes: the world day of prayer for the unborn, for the child, for the Third World, for the hungry, for those suffering political persecution, for those undergoing economic oppression, for cancer relief, for the papacy, for the laity, for the campaign for literacy—and so forth. One can well imagine a possible argument in favour of a whole

'Church year of theme Sundays' in terms of which the appearance of the Sunday liturgy, in many ways so insipid, would be reinvested with a fresh relevance. Those assisting at Mass would be confronted through the agency of the theme Sundays with our world's thronging problems, problems which are not supposed to pass the Christian believer by but on the contrary to lay heavy on his heart of all hearts. Are not the problems of, for example, the handicapped, minorities, refugees, a matter for the concern of the community of Jesus Christ? Are these themes not perforce to have their echo in the liturgical assembly of Christians? Could not this be the way to re-establish the lost continuity between liturgy and life?

To be sure it would not suffice for this purpose merely to mention the theme in a bidding prayer or touch on it in a sermon. More than this, the special cause should where possible govern the entire Eucharistic celebration of its appointed day: and indeed this is already often the case in practice. It should find a resonance in all the texts and hymns of the liturgy and so find its way into the thinking and feeling of those taking part. But it is less the worry that there may not be enough Sundays in the year to accommodate all such legitimate causes, and more the dubious view of liturgy that emerges these days in the special purpose Sundays and the arguments of their supporters, that makes a more rigorous consideration of their validity desirable.

If in what now follows we reject the abuses involved in this development, abuses so abundantly bestowed on the Christian Sunday and its Eucharistic liturgy by these special projects and themes, this should not be understood as disdain or contempt for the concerns and themes themselves. Someone who expresses himself as against a 'Traffic Safety Sunday' or a Sunday 'day of world-wide prayer for drug addicts' is not *eo ipso* an opponent of traffic safety or a saboteur of the fight against narcotics.

3. OBFUSCATION OF SUNDAY AS THE DAY OF THE LORD

An initial objection against theme Sundays turns on the danger that they all too easily obscure the true character of Sunday as a liturgical day. Sunday's place as the first day of the week is not given it by some special cause; it is grounded in the most crucial actions of God in saving history. The Constitution on the Liturgy of the Second Vatican Council formulated this theological perspective in the following way: 'By an apostolic tradition which took its origin from the very day of Christ's resurrection, the Church celebrates the paschal mystery every eighth day; with good reason, then, this bears the name of the Lord's day or the day of the Lord.'[15] The climax of God's saving activity in the resurrection of Christ, the passover of Jesus and with him the whole creation, from death to life, is what gives the *dies dominica* its pre-eminent position. The Council's document does not hesitate to call Sunday 'the foundation and nucleus of the whole liturgical year' and to characterise it as 'the original feast day'.[16]

Yet as such a feast day it must be increasingly called into question wherever it is overlaid with themes and ideas that can furnish no grounds for its celebration.[17] Neither universal mission nor (frequently unforthcoming) vocations nor (the problematic issue of) safety on the roads can be the foundation for the celebration of the eighth day. In so far as this is so it must be asked whether the tying in of contemporary concerns with the very word 'Sunday' does not in itself indicate a theological devaluation of the Lord's day. In place of ever new Sundays with their 'projects' would it not be preferable to revitalise a fundamentally necessary dimension of the spirituality of the Christian Sunday? In the pursuit of theme Sundays does not a considerable decline in the, pastorally and spiritually so vital, value of Sunday come out into the open?

4. THE DANGER OF USING SUNDAY FOR WRONG ENDS

As the brief review at the start of this article indicates, the proliferation of special purpose Sundays brings with it a growing tendency to allow the Sunday Eucharist to be more and more strongly determined in its character by these themes. As a result of this development the ideal cause of a celebration can come to appear one where the special projects twists and turns throughout its course like Ariadne's thread.

But is it really the object of the Sunday Eucharistic assembly to confront people, first and foremost, with a problem of Church or society? Does not the community live, from first to last, by the encounter with its Lord? Must it not look towards him, listen to him in his Word and receive his Gifts? Does not the decisive actuality of the worship of God lie here? If Sunday as a whole is the celebration of the paschal mystery, then does not the Sunday Mass actualise the Easter event in an unsurpassable way as a 'memorial of the death and resurrection of Christ'?[18] This is the yardstick to be applied in the face of the tendency to overwhelm the congregation at Sunday Mass with a flood of information about a theme and harass them in their capacity as possible donors of cash.[19]

5. THE FRAGMENTATION OF LIFE

Finally there remains one question, in reflecting on the ecclesiastical special purpose Sunday, which does not stem from liturgical considerations. Are special purpose days and years (brought in for the most part in an arbitrary and bureaucratic fashion) of any use to man in his life and relationships with others? Parallels to these periodic calls on our attention with regard to special causes (worthy enough in themselves) are not hard to find in the life of society: the day of the tree, the day of milk, days for world health and sharing of goods, the year of the woman and the year of the child. Are such cause-bound days and years, organised, propagated, borne in as they see on people from without, really fair to human living? Do they not carry with them a certain attempt to divide up the reality of living and to tear it into fragments? And if so is anything really gained outside of a brief smash and grab raid on our attention? The same may perhaps be suspected of ecclesiastically approved causes when they likewise are given their own special days in the calendar.

6. A LITURGICAL CONSIDERATION OF THE IDEA OF THE GOOD CAUSE

One can glimpse a better way than that of the special purpose Sundays where it is a matter of taking up causes that genuinely emerge in an organic way out of the life of the community. For instance a concern with the 'promotion of vocations' becomes a quite concrete affair for a parish at a priestly ordination, priestly jubilee, a religious profession, a jubilee of religious profession, and so on. In this connection there might well be a liturgy whose object is determined by the special occasion; and here the form of a 'liturgy of the Word' may well be seen as especially suitable. Not because the liturgy of the Word is something inferior to the Mass but because in the course of liturgical history very rich forms of celebrating it have arisen.

Particular concerns can also find expression in the votive Mass, i.e., celebrations of Mass permeated by some appropriate primary motif. These have a traditional place on weekdays, especially outside the great liturgical seasons. At an earlier stage of the historical evolution, the motives underlying the celebration of votive Masses were what gave an impulse to holding the Eucharist during the course of the working week, something not then generally the custom.

As to what concerns the making of such 'occasional' Mass celebrations, the composition of texts and hymn material, it can here only be pointed out that in a liturgical perspective a mere incidental mention of the occasion will not suffice. The incorporation of the primary motif suggested by the occasion in the whole liturgical act must follow certain inner demands of the liturgy itself; this makes the preparation of such liturgies no easy matter.[20] Including a reflection on the occasion to hand should not lead to the mere juxtaposition of heterogeneous elements. It seems a questionable practice, therefore, to thematise the variable elements in the celebration of Mass according to the current *Ordo* (for example, introduction, greeting, Kyrie, bidding prayers) and yet leave the given elements in the Missal as they are.

Finally it should be asked whether it would not in fact suffice for many occasions to leave well alone the texts for proclamation and prayer, not to mention the hymns, laid down for the Sunday, and simply to allude to the special purpose in the Prayer of the Faithful.[21] Would not a deepened and living celebration of the Memorial of the Lord in its Sunday form help achieve the very aims that the special purpose Sunday was created to serve?

Translated by Anton Nichols

Notes

1. See Rescript of the Congregation of Rites, 14.4.1926: *AAS* 19 (1927) 23f. The prayers of the Mass for the Propagation of the Faith should be added to those of the Sunday in question. The sermon should be concerned, though not exclusively, with mission and should encourage the faithful to become members of the Pontifical Society for the Propagation of the Faith. A plenary indulgence was attached to the reception of communion and prayer for the conversion of unbelievers. Where the alms of the faithful were collected for this purpose, this was not to prejudice other, possibly mandatory, collections.

2. Additional indulgences in conformity with the Decree of the College of Penitentiaries of 30.18.1934: *AAS* 26 (1934) 526f. Further mention of world mission days may be found in the norms for the implementation of the Decree of the Second Vatican Council *Ad gentes divinitus* of 6.8.1966: *AAS* 58 (1966) 783. For the use of the votive Mass *Pro evangelizatione populorum* see the *Missale Romanum* 1975, 813.

3. Pius XII, Apostolic constitution *Exsul familia* of 1.8.1952: *AAS* 44 (1952) 702. Also, see the instruction *De pastorali migratorum cura* of 22.8.1969: *AAS* 61 (1969) 627.

4. Decree of the Second Vatican Council *Inter mirifica*, § 18: *AAS* 56 (1964) 151.

5. Instruction of the Papal Commission for the Means of Communication *Communio et progressio* of 23.5.1971, Nos. 167 and 171: *AAS* 63 (1971) 649f. From time to time this Commission also published other liturgical texts in various vernaculars; this in disregard of the Second Vatican Council's confirmation of the exclusive rights of conferences of bishops to approve liturgical texts in the bishops' local vernacular.

6. See the letter of the papal Secretary of State of 23.1.1964 to the Congregation for the Formation of the Clergy, referred to by the *Ratio fundamentalis institutionis sacerdotalis* of 6.1.1970 (note 56): *AAS* 62 (1970) 337. See also the address of Pope Paul VI of 11.4.1964: *AAS* 65 (1964) 396f.

7. See the *Ordo Missae celebrande et Divini Officii persolvendi secundum Calendarium Romanum Generale pro anno liturgico* 1979-80 (Citta del Vaticano 1979) 53. According to the earlier provisions the day fell on the Second Sunday after Easter; according to those in force at present on the Fourth Sunday of Eastertide.

8. See note 7 in the *Ordo* mentioned, 12.

9. See J. A. Jungmann 'Das kirchliche Fest nach Idee und Grenze' in *Liturgisches Erbe und pastorale Gegenwart* (Innsbruck 1960) 502-526.

10. *Calendarium Romanum* No. 5, Edito typica (Citta del Vaticano 1969) 66ff.

11. See *Schweizerische Kirchenzeitung* 144 (1976) 668f.

12. See A. J. Chupungco 'Easter Sunday in Latin Patristic Literature' *Notitiae* 16 (1980) 94.

13. Thus for example in the dioceses of the Federal Republic of Germany: see *Kirchliches Amtsblatt*, Paderborn, 122 (1979) 173.

14. See on this D. Eissing 'Sonntagsfeier in Gefahr' *Gottesdienst* 10 (1976) 123-127; K. Richter 'Die liturgische Feier des Sonntags' *Theologie und Glaube* 68 (1978) 23-39.

15. Constitution of the Second Vatican Council *Sacrosanctum Concilium* of 4.12.1963, § 106: *AAS* 56 (1964) 126.

16. From this it is clear that according to the rubrics of the liturgical calendar Sunday enjoys a generous degree of protection, being replaceable only by great feasts and feasts of Christ's own mysteries. Even here the Sundays of Advent, Lent and Eastertide take precedence: see *Calendarium Romanum* No. 5, cited in note 10.

17. See *Célébrer l'eucharistie aujourd'hui*, edited by the Commission Interdiocésaine de Pastorale Liturgique (CIPL) (Brussels 1978) pp. 105ff.; also available as *Lettre pastorale des Evêques de la partie francophone de Belgique* (Brussels 1978) 6ff.

18. *Sacrosanctum Concilium*, § 47: *AAS* (1964) 113, cited in note 15.

19. For 'thematised celebrations of Mass' with a notably moralising tendency in the French diocesan liturgies of the eighteenth century, see P. Jounel 'Les Missels diocésains français du 18e siècle' *La Maison-Dieu* 141 (1980) 95ff.

20. See H. Rennings 'Modelle thematischer Messgestaltung?' *Liturgisches Jahrbuch* 21 (1971) 117-119; P. Harnoncourt 'Motivmessen und Votivmessen' *Gottesdienst* 8 (1974) 121-123; id. 'Thematische Messfeiern. "Motivmessen" und "Votivmessen" mit den neuen liturgischen Büchern' *Lebendige Seelsorge* 26 (1975) 286-291; A. Haüssling 'Messhaüfigkeit und "Motivmessen"' *Gemeinde im Herrenmahl* ed. T. Maas-Ewerd and K. Richter, (Freiburg ²1976) 143-149; H. B. Meyer 'Zuerst der Sonntag. Die Feier des "Herrentages" und die Anliegen der "Zwecksonntage" sinnvoll verbinden' *Gottesdienst* 12 (1978) 185ff.; see also the articles mentioned in note 14 above.

21. See also *Célébrer l'eucharistie aujourd'hui*, cited in note 17.

Contributors

ANDRÉ AUBRY was born in 1927. He studied ethnosociology at the Institut Oriental at Beirut and at the Sorbonne in Paris. He also studied liturgy at the Institut Supérieur de Liturgie in Paris. He was an assistant priest in Paris from 1961 until 1969 and taught at the Instituto de Liturgia Pastoral of CELAM at Medellín, Colombia from 1969 until 1972. Since 1974, he has co-ordinated studies at the Instituto de Asesoría Antropológica para la Región Maya, A.C. (INAREMAC) at San Cristóbal de Las Casas Chiapas in Mexico. He has written three books and several articles on the themes dealt with in this article: *Un peuple en fête* (Paris 1967); *Les Temps de la liturgie est-elle passé?* (Paris 1968), see Chapters VI, VII and VIII especially; *Una iglesia sin parroquias* (Mexico 1974), see Chapter 7 especially; 'Imagination in the Liturgy and Christian Feasts' *Concilium* Vol 9, No 5 (Nov. 1969); 'Lenguage litúrgico y iniciación cristiana, tu misma palabra te descubre', *Phase* 449 (Barcelona 1970); 'El pan y la libertad', *Christus* 470 (Mexico 1975); 'Todos somos indigenas' *Contacto* 12, 4 (Mexico 1975); 'Los campesinos en las luchas de liberación' *Apuntes de Lectura* 5 (INAREMAC) (San Cristóbal de Las Casas 1979). He has also published several books on other subjects and many articles in French, Belgian and other journals.

ANSCAR CHUPUNGCO OSB, is a monk of the Abbey of Our Lady of Montserrat (Manila); President of the Pontifical Liturgical Institute (Rome); professor of liturgical history and liturgical adaptation; consultor to the Sacred Congregation for the Sacraments and Divine Worship (Section Divine Worshop); and a member of the editorial committee for the liturgy section of *Concilium*. His books include: *Towards a Filipino Liturgy* (Manila 1976); *The Cosmic Elements of Christian Passover* (Rome 1977).

IRÉNÉE-HENRI DALMAIS OP, was born in 1914 at Vienne, France, and ordained in 1945. He studied at the Saulchoir theological faculty, at Lyons University and at the Sorbonne. He has been professor of eastern liturgies at the Paris Higher Liturgical Institute since 1956. Among his works are *Initiation à la Liturgie* (Paris 1958), *Saints et sanctuaries d'Orient* (Paris 1968) and, with others: *Shalom: Chrétiens à l'écoute des grandes religions* (Paris 1972) and *Liturgies d'Orient* (Paris 1980).

LLUÍS DUCH was born in Barcelona and is a monk of the Abbey of Montserrat. A doctor of theology and member of the Institute of Anthropology of Barcelona, his published works include: *Ciencia de la Religión y mito* (1978); *La experiencia religiosa en el contexto de la cultura contemporánea* (1979); *De la religió a la religió popular* (1980) as well as numerous articles in *Qüestiones de Vida Cristiana*, *Serra d'Oro*, *Studia monástica*, *Perspectiva social* and other journals.

PETER EICHER was born at Winterthur, Switzerland, in 1943. He studied philosophy, literature, history and theology at the universities of Fribourg and Tübingen, gaining his doctorate in philosophy in 1969 and in theology in 1976. From 1971 to 1974 he was a research assistant for the Deutsche Forschungsgemeinschaft, from

1974 to 1977 a research assistant at Tübingen, and since 1977 he has been professor of systematic theology at Paderborn. He is married with five children. His publications include: *Die anthropologische Wende: Karl Rahners philosophischer Weg vom Wesen des Menschen zur personalen Existenz* (Fribourg 1970); *Solidarischer Glaube* (Düsseldorf 1975); *Offenbarung—Prinzip neuzeitlicher Theologie* (Munich 1977); *Im Verborgenenoffenbar* (Essen 1978); *Der Herr gibt's den Seinen im Schlaf* (Munich 1980); *Theologie—eine Einführung in das Studium* (Munich 1980). He edited the volume *Gottesvorstellung und Gesellschaftsentwicklung* (Munich 1979) and has contributed to periodicals numerous articles on religious studies, philosophy, contemporary history and theology.

JULIEN POTEL was born in Alfortville in the suburbs of Paris in 1922. He was ordained priest for the Mission de France in 1949 and was for ten years curate at Colombes, a working-class parish in the Paris suburbs. He is specialising in sociology and is taking courses at the Institut Catholique at the Sorbonne in Paris. He has taken part in seminars of the Sociology of Religions group. Abbé Potel has done research into the changing character of priests in France which resulted in three books published in 1967 and 1977 and has also written on popular attitudes to baptism and to death and funerals. He is a member of the Association Française de Sociologie Religieuse and of the International Conference for the Sociology of Religions.

HEINRICH RENNINGS was born in 1926 in Moers-Niederhein. In 1955 he became a priest of the diocese of Münster and after studies in Münster, Innsbruck and Paris began theological teaching in 1965. In the years from 1966 to 1974 he was an assistant professor in the Liturgical Institute in Trier. Since 1975 he has been professor of liturgical studies in the theological faculty at Paderborn. Editor of the series *Lebendiger Gottesdienst* (Münster 1961-   ), he has contributed articles to *Liturgisches Jahrbuch*, *Theologie und Glaube* and *Gottesdienst*.

THOMAS TALLEY was born in Gainesville, Texas, in 1924. He is a priest of the Episcopal Church. After ten years as a parish priest in Texas, he undertook graduate study and received the ThD at the General Theological Seminary in 1969. He has taught at Nashotah House in Wisconsin, at Notre Dame University in Indiana, and has been professor of liturgics at the General Theological Seminary (New York City) since 1971. He has contributed to several reference volumes and is the author of articles which have appeared in liturgical journals in the United States and Europe, among them, 'History and Eschatology in the Primitive Pascha' in *Worship* 47 (1973). 'The Origin of Lent at Alexandria', presented to the liturgy Master Theme at the Oxford Patristic Conference in 1979, appears this year in *Studia Patristica*.

ADALBERT DE VOGÜÉ OSB, was born in Paris in 1924 and has been a monk of the Abbey of Pierre-qui-vire since 1944. He has taught for ten years at San Anselmo in Rome. Firmly attached to the Catholic tradition as he is, he does not approve of certain tendencies to be found in *Concilium*. His published works include *La Règle du Maître* (1964), *La Règle de saint Benoît* (1972) together with a *Commentaire historique* and a *Commentaire doctrinal* on the latter (1977), and the *Dialogues* of St Gregory. Some of his articles are gathered together in *Autour de S. Benoit* (1975) and *S. Benoît. Sa vie et sa Règle* (1980).

SIMON DE VRIES was born in Denver, Colorado, in 1921, and educated at Calvin College and Seminary, Grand Rapids, Michigan, and at Union Theological Seminary in New York (ThD 1958), with graduate study in Leiden and Tübingen. He was ordained minister in the United Presbyterian Church in the USA. He was resident scholar at the Ecumenical Institute for Advance Theological Studies, Jerusalem, 1973 and visiting professor at King's College, London, 1978 and now teaches at the Methodist Theological School in Delaware, Ohio. His published books are: *Bible and Theology in The Netherlands* (Wageningen 1968); *Yesterday, Today and Tomorrow* (Grand Rapids and London 1975); *Prophet Against Prophet* (Grand Rapids 1978). He has also written numerous scholarly articles and reviews in a variety of journals and composite works, including essays on 'Chronology of the Old Testament' and 'Calendar' in *The Interpreter's Bible*.

Publications from T. & T. Clark

NICENE AND POST-NICENE FATHERS OF THE CHRISTIAN CHURCH: SECOND SERIES

Translated into English with Prolegomena and Explanatory Notes under the editorial supervision of Phillip Schaff and Henry Wace

Complete Catalogue free on request.

T. & T. CLARK LIMITED
36 George Street
Edinburgh EH2 2LQ
Scotland